# Rethinking Discipleship

Alan Pue

# Rethinking Discipleship

## Why Christian Schooling Matters

ACSI
STRONGER TOGETHER

Purposeful Design Publications is the publishing division of the Association of Christian Schools International (ACSI) and is committed to the ministry of Christian school education, to enable Christian educators and schools worldwide to effectively prepare students for life. As the publisher of textbooks, trade books, and other educational resources within ACSI, Purposeful Design Publications strives to produce biblically sound materials that reflect Christian scholarship and stewardship and that address the identified needs of Christian schools around the world.

The views expressed in this publication are those of the author, and they may not necessarily represent the position of the Association of Christian Schools International.

Unless otherwise marked, all Scripture quotations are taken from The Holy Bible, English Standard Version. Copyright 2001 by Crossway Bibles, a division of Good News Publishers.

Printed in the United States of America

26 25 24 23 22 21      2 3 4 5 6 7

Pue, Alan
*Rethinking Discipleship: Why Christian schooling matters*
ISBN 978-1-58331-560-6 Catalog #6678
eISBN 978-1-58331-561-3 Catalog #e6678

Designer: Lisa Ruppert
Editor: John Conaway

Purposeful Design Publications
*A Division of ACSI*
731 Chapel Hills Dr. • Colorado Springs, CO 80920
Care Team: 800-367-0798 • www.acsi.org

This book is dedicated to Dr. Al Janney, Dr. Verle and
Mrs. Lucile Ackerman, Lynn and Janet Warner, and all the others at
New Testament Baptist Church who encouraged me as a young man
and ignited my passion for Christ and Christian schooling.

# Contents

# Foreword

Before becoming president of the Association of Christian Schools International (ACSI), I had the privilege of serving in two of the great churches in America—First Baptist Church of Orlando, Florida; and, Prestonwood Baptist Church, Plano (North Dallas), Texas. And, during this time that spanned thirty-two years I was blessed to serve with two amazing pastors and leaders—Pastor Jim Henry, in Orlando, and Pastor Jack Graham in Dallas. I have witnessed firsthand a variety of training practices provided by these two churches, especially ones geared to children and youth. I have also been blessed by these two pastors' love and priority for kingdom education provided by their two schools, of which I served.

Early in my transition from public school teaching and coaching to Christian school teaching, coaching, and administration, I heard about Dr. Alan Pue. I admired Dr. Pue from a distance usually through reading one of his journal or book publications or attending one of his seminars at a conference. The one word I would choose to describe my respect for Dr. Pue is *wisdom*. The consistent thread through his articles, books, and speeches was always wisdom. And not just theoretical-based wisdom, but experiential-based wisdom. When he spoke or wrote, his practical wisdom and application came from a deep reservoir of experience. I liked learning from a leader who had been in the same trenches God had called me to. I also liked Dr. Pue, the person who I now call Alan, my friend.

Through conversations, serving together on nonprofit boards, and collaborating on like-minded missions, I discovered another word describing my friend Alan—courage. Wisdom is great, but Alan has the courage to convey this knowledge, understanding, and insight. I have experienced it up close most recently when our board of directors selected him to facilitate ACSI's strategic planning process. His wisdom helped us categorize what our organization needed to review, but it was his courage that forced us to ask the tough questions. As I read through this book, *Rethinking Discipleship*, I found myself once again valuing Alan's wisdom and courage.

From the preface to the concluding chapter, *Rethinking Discipleship* deals with the questions that should be front and center for every parent, pastor, educator, and parachurch ministry. The initial question, and quite frankly the one that pulled my curiosity strings throughout the entire book, asked—what does it take to flourish as a follower of Jesus Christ in the kind of world we live in today? There are a lot of important questions we need to be asking, but few, if any, are more critical than what it takes to flourish as a follower of Jesus Christ. Knowing Alan as long as I have, this is not the first time he has asked this question. He has devoted his life to what I consider the noblest of all causes—training and passing on our faith to the next generation. He has eloquently delivered this flourishing question in churches, schools, universities, and parachurch ministries. But never have I sensed Alan's plea to get our attention as much as I did when reading this book.

Alan's blend of wisdom and courage is undoubtedly what I consider the major strength of this book. He asks the readers to consider the best way to fulfill the responsibility of training our children. More specifically, Alan is challenging us to rethink our approach to the discipleship of our children. He urges us to alter the training paradigms that have long been used by parents, churches, and schools. Characteristic of Alan's style, again the blend of wisdom and courage, he spends no time in the shallow waters. He wastes no time in offering pragmatic steps to transform our discipleship models. He does not just preach another sermon on why we need to change how we train our children; he walks us through specific ideas, strategies, and plans.

*Rethinking Discipleship* is not for the faint of heart. It is not another feel-good book for parents and pastors. Alan does not tiptoe in the least. And he is specifically straightforward when addressing our children's education. Alan, the scholar, theologian, and practitioner, positions his claims with empirically based research. His arguments are not based on emotion or personal preference, but rather on educational methodology and philosophical assumptions. He provides reasonable and persuasive evidence to support his assumptions. He respectfully challenges those in leadership positions at churches to rethink the correlation between education and disciple making. His appeal is for parents and churches to recognize their need for one another, as well as for additional training and education options for their children. He argues that without a truly Christian approach to education, then producing children who flourish for the cause of Christ will continue to languish.

One would think that Alan's claims and arguments represent a one-sided view in favor of Christian schools. As a fellow Christian educator one of my favorite parts of this book is the repudiation of how many Christian schools teach and train their students. I am deeply grateful for how Alan spurs Christian schools to engage in real-life faith training practices. His petition to Christian school leaders and faculty members to change their pedagogical approach is as strong as the other claims in the book. In other words, he does not endorse Christian schooling with blinders on. He is as forthright about Christian schools making adaptive level change as he is about countering the longstanding positions against sending our children to Christian schools.

I am honored to write the foreword for *Rethinking Discipleship*. But not just because of my friendship with the author, Alan Pue. Rather, because I believe this book addresses the most important factor facing Christianity today—the discipleship-making process. This book elevates above the many opinions of those for or against Christian schooling. This book fearlessly enters the debate of Christian schooling by focusing on God's Word. Allowing God's Word to inform us on one of the greatest mandates in all of Scripture is at the heart of the author. This does not surprise me about my friend, Dr. Alan Pue. I believe that this book answers the fundamental question—what does it take to flourish as a follower of Jesus Christ in the kind of world we live in today?

Larry Taylor, Ph.D.
President/CEO, ACSI
President-Emeritus, Prestonwood Christian Academy School System
Author, *Running With the Horses*

# It's Time to Flourish

Think for a moment. In one hundred years, what legacy do you want to leave for the students that sit in your classrooms? ACSI wants to come alongside you and help your school community flourish how God intends—biblically.

ACSI has been leading Christ-centered education toward excellence for more than 40 years, always seeking to understand what truly impacts and improves a Christian school. Through a multi-year research endeavor, ACSI identified thirty-five constructs that support five primary domains, which create a school community consisting of healthy spiritual, emotional, and cultural characteristics. This research was validated by a rigorous independent review sponsored by Cardus and blossomed into the ACSI Flourishing Initiative.

*Rethinking Discipleship* advances Christ-centered education by encouraging intentional biblical discipleship. Additionally, this book fits into the Flourishing domain of purpose, focusing on the spiritual formation of a child's faith and the holistic teaching of developing a child emotionally and spiritually.

To learn more, please visit **acsi.org/flourishing**.

# Preface

"What do you want? That's the question. It is the first, last, and most fundamental question of Christian discipleship." So argues James K. A. Smith in his thought-provoking book *You Are What You Love: The Spiritual Power of Habit*. Personally ponder that question for a moment. Be honest. What is it that you really want for yourself: power, prestige, a nice home in a nice place, a fast car, a beautiful wife or handsome husband, the freedom to travel, kids who will make you proud, lots of friends? I could go on with this list, but I know you catch my drift.

You might even say, "I want to be a devoted follower of Jesus Christ." Indeed, if you are reading this book you would probably say something like that. And if you are a parent you would likely also say something like, "I want my kids to also be devoted followers of Jesus Christ."

But here's the question. What is the likelihood that either of those two things will actually happen? Does that devotion just occur? Do people just wake up one day and find themselves devoted followers of Jesus Christ? Will that devotion survive crisis or disappointment or the disapproval of those in the cultural ocean in which we swim on a daily basis, or even perhaps persecution? What if your job is at risk or that coveted promotion? How will that desire fare in the face of ridicule? Tough questions to be sure. Given our current cultural moment, not unrealistic however.

Now ask, and again be honest, how about your children? How will they fare in that kind of environment? What does it take to prepare them, and yourself for that matter, to walk in this world as genuine followers of Jesus Christ, to face the daily barrage of messages, messages designed by those who have something to sell and who understand the power of images and words to make the sale? What does it take to flourish as a follower of Jesus Christ in that kind of world?

That is the fundamental question of this book. It is an unavoidable question because preparing our children for life as followers of Christ in this fallen world is among our most fundamental responsibilities, and as I will point out later, it is a responsibility for which our Lord will hold us to account.

Parenting and shepherding have always been difficult jobs. Our current cultural context certainly makes that task even more challenging. No more so, however, than parenting in the world of the early church or the world in which many followers of Jesus Christ live today. Think of what it would be like to live in China or Iran or North Korea or Turkey or Pakistan or Saudi Arabia or even much of modern-day Europe. In fact, rare have been the times and places that living for and loving Christ have been easy. In all of those times and places, however, the genuine followers of Christ found a way. That task is ours as well.

How best to fulfill our responsibility is the second question that I set out to answer in this book. If, as Smith declares, "we are what we want," then how can we create the context in which our children can best decide the better answer to the question, What do I want?

If Smith is right that "our wants and longings and desires are at the core of our identity; the wellspring from which our actions and behavior flow," how then can we learn to "align our loves and longings with His—to want what God wants, to desire what God desires, to hunger and thirst after God and crave a world where He is all in all"?

In responding to those questions, I can tell you it takes more than the forty-seven hours a year that the average child or young person who attends an evangelical church spends in attending services at that church during the course of a year (and I doubt that number is much different in Catholic or mainline Protestant families). It takes more than the fifteen minutes a day that the average dad spends in conversation with his children. And it surely takes more than just learning a handful of facts and Bible verses—much more.

It takes, as I intend to show throughout this book, immersion in a particular kind of culture—an intentional, intensive, and yes, ongoing and incidental interaction with a particular team of persons, those who themselves love our Lord and desire to align their own lives with His person and purposes. It requires a daily, ongoing, systematic effort—not the current episodic, sporadic, disjointed efforts currently employed in too many homes and churches. It's time, actually past time, to rethink our approach to the discipleship of our children.

I hope that what I have to say in the following chapters causes you to stop and reflect and hopefully to embrace what I believe to be a better and more biblical way forward.

In a brief letter written near the end of his life, John, the beloved disciple, shares his heart with someone he calls "the elect lady." To her he writes, "I rejoiced greatly to find some of your children walking in the truth, just as we were commanded by the Father." Seeing our children walk in the truth is something I desire, as I am sure you do as well. It is my prayer that this book will provide some specific ideas, and the encouragement to act on those ideas, so that we can, as did John, rejoice to see our children walking in the truth.

# Introduction

We are at war. And I'm not talking about the ongoing conflicts in the Middle East, or the trade war with China, or the nasty political infighting that characterizes so much of our political life here in the United States. It isn't a war aimed at acquiring territory or resources. It isn't a war driven by a desire to protect or promote democracy. No blood is being shed, but lives are being lost. No enemy soldiers carrying weapons are roaming our streets, but the battle rages in virtually every neighborhood and community in our country.

No, this isn't war as we typically think of war. Rather, it is a war for the hearts, minds, and lives of our children and young people. The war is real, however, and we are losing—badly.

In April 1983, the National Commission on Education appointed by President Ronald Reagan released a long-awaited report on the state of education in the United States. In the introduction to that report, titled, "A Nation at Risk," the authors made the following observations:

> Our nation is at risk. Our once unchallenged preeminence in commerce, industry, science, and technological innovation is being overtaken by competitors throughout the world. This report is concerned with only one of the many causes and dimensions of the problem, but it is one that undergirds American prosperity, security and civility. We report to the American people that while we can take justifiable pride in what our schools and colleges have historically accomplished and contributed to the United States and the well-being of its people, the educational foundations of our society are currently being eroded by a rising tide of mediocrity that threatens our very future as a Nation and a people. What was unimaginable a generation ago has begun to occur as others are matching and surpassing our educational attainments.

Now I ask you to pay careful attention to what the authors say next. "If an unfriendly foreign power had attempted to impose on America the mediocre educational performance that exists today, we might well have viewed it as an act of war. As it stands, we have allowed this to happen to ourselves. . . . We have, in effect, been committing an act of unthinking, unilateral educational disarmament. . . . Our society and its educational institutions seem to have lost sight of the basic purpose of schooling and the high expectations and disciplined efforts needed to attain them."[1]

When one looks at the current performance data, it would appear that not much has changed in our nation's schools over the last thirty-plus years. We are still very much at risk, and we seem increasingly unaware of the "basic purpose of schooling" or of the "high expectations and disciplined effort needed to attain them."

The focus of this book is not, however, to ponder the continuing decline of our American public schools. Rather, its purpose is to consider a similar situation facing the American evangelical church, the "we" I mentioned in the opening paragraph. Consider the impact of just a few edits in the language. "*The evangelical church in America is at risk. Our once unchallenged preeminence in building the religious and moral foundation for our country has been lost. Indeed, that foundation is cracking in ways unimaginable just a generation ago.*" This book is concerned with only one of the many causes and dimensions of that problem, but it is one that undergirds the current and future church.

The rich history of faith that has characterized the evangelical church in America and that has allowed the church to have such a great impact on America's spiritual and moral fiber is currently being eroded by a rising tide of secular thought that has taken root in the hearts and minds of those who sit in the pews of even the most theologically conservative churches in this country. Indeed, current research on the religious and spiritual lives of American young people demonstrates just how thoroughly secularized they have become.[2]

Unfortunately, attempts to explain this decline in theological awareness and spiritual vitality have failed to identify the real villain. We have certainly pinpointed a number of the villain's henchmen, or perhaps I should say, henchpersons. The list is a familiar one: Hollywood, government run amuck, media, social media, and those crazy colleges and universities.

As Walt Kelly presciently observed in his *Pogo* comic strip, however, "We have met the enemy and he is us." As it stands, we have allowed this to happen to ourselves. We have, in effect, been committing an act of unthinking, unilateral, spiritual disarmament, and I believe it is time to acknowledge that reality. Thus, it is the purpose of this book to address the historical, cultural, and theological reasons for this precipitous decline and to offer a way forward.

To state it bluntly, I believe that our current approach to the education of our children and young people is flawed based as it is upon questionable methodology, false philosophical assumptions, and a complete repudiation of the existence of God, who acts in the affairs of His creation. Sadly, however, few parents and pastors in our evangelical churches seem to grasp the implications of that reality. Public schooling is, and has been, such an integral part of our cultural and historical reality that people find it hard to believe that there is a problem, much less a problem of the size and scope I am suggesting by my statement that *we are at war.*

Indeed, for a lot of people that statement will seem dangerously reckless. To which I would reply by saying, "Dangerous, yes, but in the same way that poking a wasp's nest might be dangerous. Reckless, yes, but in the sense that disturbing the wasp's status quo might result in a painful sting. Necessary, however, in the same sense that a wasp nest left undisturbed will likely continue to inflict pain on those who are nearby."

Several years ago I came across a compelling quote from a pastor in California. He posed a question that haunts me even today. "Why are we surprised," he asked "*that when we give our children to Caesar for their education that what we get in return are Romans?*" Why indeed? It is a question, however, that we must consider if we are to have any hope of recapturing real spiritual vitality in our churches. It is certainly not the only thing we must consider, but it is one we have ignored too long and that undergiwwrds everything we are called by our Lord to accomplish in this world.

Our nation was at risk educationally in 1983. The evidence underlying that conclusion was based on objective research. Unfortunately, similar research tells us little has changed over the last thirty-five years. Sadly, the church in our present time is equally at risk. The evidence supporting that assertion is equally objective and equally compelling. Yet those in leadership of our churches seem reluctant to consider rethinking our approach to disciple making, especially the discipleship of our children and young people. That just doesn't make sense to me.

My purpose in writing this book is in large part to make the case that the church has abandoned its biblical mandate and historic practice of making disciples, of which the daily education of children played a central role. I intend to show that we surrendered that mandate for cultural and political reasons, and once having done so we have lacked the conviction and courage to take back the responsibility given to us by our Lord. It is time—past time, actually—to do what we have so clearly been commanded to do and what the church for centuries saw as one of its primary responsibilities.

I have no doubt that some, perhaps many, having read only this far, are ready to set this book aside—and let me warn you at the outset that my words moving forward will likely continue to sting. Please know, however, that my goal is not simply to be provocative. As the author of Proverbs reminds us, "Faithful are the wounds of a friend" (Proverbs 27:6). In that sense, as Derek Kidner observes, "David shirked his duty to Adonijah his son ('he had not displeased him at anytime in saying, 'Why hast thou done so?') and it cost that son his life."[3]

Knowing that some of what I have to say will smart a bit, I plead with you to continue reading. While you may or may not agree with what I have to say, I entreat you to give what I have to say your full attention. Don't simply dismiss my argument out of hand because it doesn't align with your current thinking. At least be like the noble Bereans, who after hearing Paul preach, spent time "examining the Scriptures daily to see if these things were so" (Acts 17:11).

## Jesus Makes Our Mission Clear

On a windswept hillside in the region of Galilee, north of Jerusalem, our Lord meets with His disciples one final time before ascending into heaven. I suspect it was a somber gathering as the disciples pondered the future without the presence of their Lord. The promise of the Holy Spirit was real, but had not yet been experienced. They knew that everything had changed, but they didn't quite understand the full implications of what they would soon encounter and what they must do.

Into this air of uncertainty Jesus speaks with clarity: "All authority in heaven and on earth has been given to me. Go therefore and make disciples of all nations, baptizing them in the name of the Father and of the Son and of the Holy Spirit, teaching them to observe all that I have commanded you. And behold I am with you always, to the end of the age" (Matthew 28:18–20).

Somehow, we have lost sight of a full, robust meaning of that commission. This book is an attempt to once again bring clarity to the most important mission in all of human history and to the role that the church must once again play in the day-to-day education of our children and young people in fulfilling that command.

It is, as well, a plea to all of us to more fully comprehend who and what has been entrusted to us and how we must respond as good stewards of that trust.

## A Framework for a Way Forward

To present my case that Christ-centered schooling is the appropriate way for Christian parents to educate their children, I have structured my book to answer a series of questions:

- Just what did Christ mean when he said, "Make disciples"?
- What does the Bible say about the role parents play in fulfilling that mission?
- What does the Bible say about the role churches play in fulfilling that mission?
- How are schooling and disciple making two sides of the same coin?
- What is the "why" behind the "what" of schooling and disciple making?
- What should characterize our efforts to "make disciples"?
- What can we say in response to questions raised by Christian-schooling skeptics?
- Why did the church in the USA abandon its educational responsibility?
- What must we do now?

There are times I wish this could just be a fascinating conversation about some esoteric topic with little real impact on our lives and the lives of our children. That is sadly not the case. Rather, I would argue that we have reached a kind of tipping point. Will the sun still come up tomorrow if we don't respond in a timely fashion? Of course. But the landscape revealed by that rising sun will look much different if we don't soon begin taking seriously our responsibility to make disciples.

I think an observation by Rod Dreher is worth noting at this point. He writes, "The light of Christianity is flickering out all over the West. There are people alive today who may live to see the effective death of Christianity within our civilization. By God's mercy, the faith may continue to flourish in the Global South and China, but barring a dramatic reversal of current trends, it will all but disappear entirely from Europe and North America. This may not be the end of the world, but it is the end of 'a' world, and only the willfully blind would deny it. For a long time we have downplayed or ignored the signs. Now the floodwaters are upon us—and we are not ready."[4]

You may view that observation as a bit over the top. We may be in a tough time, you may say, but we've been here before, and as always, we'll find a way out. I wish it were that simple. Yes, the church has faced great challenges throughout the last 2,000 years. And yes, it always finds a way forward. Neither Dreher nor I are talking about the church universal, however. Rather as Dreher notes, this may not be the end of the world, but it is an end of "a" world, the world we have known for nearly four centuries here in the United States of America.

I'm not sure I am ready to accept an assessment that bleak. I will, however, say as forcefully as I can that if we continue to ignore our responsibility to fulfill our Lord's call to "make disciples" as we should, then yes, I would say we are likely nearing the end of an era here in our country.

Finding a solution to our current dilemma will not be achieved by pursuing a different leadership structure, worship methodology, or community outreach strategy in our churches. The problems faced by the current evangelical church in the USA are of a much deeper and more systemic nature and will be resistant to minor modifications in how we do church so that we can reach the next generation.

Permit me one final thought. We no longer live the kind of agrarian lifestyle that characterized both the Old and New Testament worlds, or for that matter, much of life on this planet until the advent of the Industrial Revolution. During those previous eras the influence of family and church was far more significant than it is today. Parents were the unquestioned authority in the home, and the church was, for the most part, the unquestioned authority in the culture. That is no longer the case.

Thus, of all the reasons I could give for writing this book, one rises above all the others, and it is an argument to which I will return repeatedly throughout these pages. As parents, you need all the help you can get if you are to effectively fulfill your calling to shepherd your children. As pastors, you need all the help you can get if you are to effectively fulfill your calling to make disciples of the children and young people in your congregation. At this moment in human history, it is time for both parents and pastors to admit a simple reality: We can't do it alone.

Like it or not, we are at war. It is a war for the hearts and minds of our children and young people. The Enemy has huge resources he has unleashed to great effect. Will we continue to sit by and watch the casualty count rise, or will we respond with all of the resources given us by our Lord? That is the question. How will we answer?

## For Reflection

1. In thinking about the declining influence of the evangelical church in American life, what, in your mind, has been the biggest contributing factor in that decline?

2. Put yourself in the crowd to whom Jesus gave the Great Commission. Now ponder the thoughts and emotions they may have experienced.

3. What is your response to the statement, "Why are we surprised that when we give our kids to Caesar for their education, that what we get in return are Romans"?

Chapter 1

## Your Mission, Should You Decide to Accept It

In the old TV show and recent movie reboot starring Tom Cruise as Ethan Hunt, superspy and lead agent for the Impossible Mission Force, every episode begins in a similar fashion. Hunt is presented with a truly difficult mission, where success will require every resource he and his team can muster and where the outcome of their efforts is dangerously uncertain. What is undeniable, however, is the cost of failure: Innocent people will die, governments will be toppled, and the world will plunge into catastrophe. So, Mr. Hunt, are you up to the task?

In a similar sense, this is what happens on that hillside in Galilee where Jesus outlines for His disciples what must have seemed an impossible mission: Wherever you go in the world, be about the business of making disciples. These were, after all, a group of beleaguered men who, as followers of the crucified Jesus, were in constant danger from both the Romans and the Sanhedrin. Knowing their fear, our Lord reminds them of two crucial facts: All authority in heaven and on earth has been given to Him, and He promises to be with them always as they go about fulfilling the mission they have been given (Matthew 28:18–20).

With those promises in mind and energized by the coming of the Holy Spirit, the gospel message explodes into the hearts and minds of people—first in Jerusalem, then Judea, Samaria, and eventually into every part of the known world. Just as Jesus had foretold,[1] these early disciples bore witness to the life, work, death, and resurrection of Jesus of Nazareth, the Christ who came to redeem a lost world.

It is a compelling story, a story of men and women who literally turn the world upside down, who do so in spite of determined opposition from both political and religious leaders willing to employ horrendous means to stop the spread of the life-transforming message of the gospel. While many in the church know the rough contours of this remarkable story, many miss a crucial element that underlies everything that happens in those early centuries as the church takes root in Europe, Asia, and Africa. It is that missing element, however, that is now putting the church at risk here in the USA, Canada, and Europe.

So, what is that missing element? To begin answering that question, let me share a recent conversation I had with a dear colleague. This colleague not long ago took a position at a growing college. His responsibilities include helping to build bridges between this college and international Christian schools. During this conversation it was impossible to miss his enthusiasm for both the college and his work.

As we talked a bit, he made an observation that summed up much of the evangelical church's understanding of the Great Commission. He was so excited that this college was more missional than most other Christian colleges—missional in the sense that they had an open-admissions policy. For my colleague this meant that the college where he served had an opportunity to share the gospel with nonbelieving students. Most pastors of most evangelical churches would likely agree to a similar understanding of the word missional.

In a very real sense, however, it is my observation that we, meaning the larger evangelical church in the USA, have equated making disciples with making converts. Thus, we tend to focus on the word "go" in the King James Version of Matthew 28:18–20 while paying less attention to the remainder of the text, in which Jesus instructs us to make disciples—first through declaration of the gospel, followed by baptism of those who respond, and then by the ongoing work of "teaching them to observe all that I have commanded you."

In simple terms this means that our work to make disciples in all nations does not end when someone prays the "sinner's prayer" or even when that person publicly submits to baptism as a sign of commitment to Christ. Those are clearly huge and crucial first steps in the process, without which the rest of the commission makes no sense. They are, however, first steps, not final steps.

As one commentator on this text in Matthew has noted, "*Matheteuo* (make disciples) is the main verb and the central command of verses 19–20, which form the closing sentence of Matthew's Gospel. The root meaning of the term refers to believing and learning. Jesus was not referring simply to believers or simply to learners, or he would have used other words. *Matheteuo* carries a beautiful combination of meanings. In this context it relates to those who place their trust in Jesus Christ and follow Him in lives of continual learning and obedience. 'If you abide in My word,' Jesus said, 'then you are truly disciples of Mine.'"[2]

"The church's mission is not simply to convert but to teach. The convert is called to a life of obedience to the Lord, and in order to obey Him it is obviously necessary to know what He requires. As already noted, a disciple is by definition a learner and follower. Therefore, studying, understanding, and obeying the whole purpose of God (Acts 20:27) is the lifelong work of every true disciple."[3]

"Jesus did not spend time teaching in order to entertain the crowds or to reveal interesting but inconsequential details about God or to set forth ideal but optional standards that God requires. His first mission was to provide salvation for those who would come to Him in faith, that is, to make disciples. His second mission was to teach God's truth to those disciples. That is the same twofold mission He gives the church."[4]

It is the core argument of this book that we, the church in the USA, are missing the mark when it comes to fulfilling that mission, and that we must be willing to acknowledge that reality, and then find a better way to move forward in fulfilling the mission to which we have been called.

## Schools, Schooling, and Disciple Making

So much more could be said, indeed, has been said, about the three verses that conclude Matthew's account of the life of Christ. What I hope is clear from the brief exposition above is this simple truth: Our disciple-making responsibility does not end when someone comes to Christ in faith. There is, without question, also a teaching-learning-acting aspect that forms a significant part of our Lord's command to make disciples. It is my argument that it is in this latter aspect of our mission where we are faltering badly.

The reasons for that failure are not difficult to identify. All we need to do is to briefly compare the ministry of Jesus and the role of parents in the context of ancient Palestine to what we see today of pastors and parents. Jesus, for example, did something completely typical of teachers in His day: He identified specific individuals and called them to "Come and follow me." Thus began a daily walk with Christ during which they received formal instruction from Him, but so much more, as they observed Him respond to a wide variety of situations.

That was important because learning is never just formal. Indeed, upon just a bit of reflection, we will all be forced to admit that much of what we learn we learn through observation. It's not just content; it's also context.

The same is true of the role that parents play when preparing their children for life. Times of family prayer and reflection on the Scriptures are crucial. Those times are, however, reinforced by the daily application of truth that children and young people observe in the lives of their parents. Again, it's not just content; it's also context. It is that daily reinforcement that makes all the difference for good or bad.

Integrating content and context was a much simpler task in a largely agrarian world. In our hyperconnected world, parents and pastors still have the potential for great influence, but that influence can be and often is diluted by the mavens of media and the daily diet of secular ideas and philosophy that influence much of educational content and practice in today's government-funded schools.

Several years ago my pastor, who is a godly man and exceptional teacher, delivered a sermon on discipling children. In that sermon he placed that discipling duty squarely on the shoulders of parents while reminding them that they could not "outsource" that responsibility to others.

I spent a good part of that Sunday afternoon pondering his thoughts and decided to respond. So I wrote him an email in which I first of all thanked him for his diligence as a teacher of the Word. I also, however, challenged him with this thought. I said, "Pastor you said in your sermon that parents can't outsource the discipling of their children. Here's reality, however. Every Monday morning, every parent who has school-age children in our church outsources the discipling of their children to someone else the moment they send them off to school." It is simple, really, because in the modern world we inhabit, unlike the agrarian world of ancient Israel:

- *Schooling is discipleship*
- *Discipleship requires schooling*

Indeed, one of the primary purposes of schooling at all times and in all places has been the transmission of culture from one generation to the next—and culture includes beliefs, values, and other elements that shape the whole person, not just the intellect. To believe that schooling is focused only on teaching children and young people the skills that they need to function in the workplace is to view schooling through a very naïve, limited lens.

Of course we want our children and young people prepared to become contributing members of our country, and of course teaching them to read, to compute, to grasp the contours of history, geography, the sciences, and to appreciate great literature and music is part of that task. There is, however, more—much more—to their preparation for life in the world than the ability to understand the difference between a verb, noun, adjective, and adverb.

Unless our children also understand all of those disciplines in the light of God's Word, they may possess some understanding of the relevant content, but they will never grasp the real meaning of that content nor develop true wisdom and discernment about how best to apply what they are learning to their day-to-day lives as followers of Jesus Christ.

To believe otherwise is to embrace a view of the world in which God is not sovereign over all things. Such a thought would have been utterly inconceivable to the authors of the sixty-six books that we collectively call the Bible. To them He is the King of kings and Lord of lords. He is, as the psalmist declares, "high above all nations, and his glory above the heavens" (Psalm 113:4). When we submit our understanding of the world and our place in the world to any higher authority than the One who declared Himself to be "I am," then we have deposed the King from His rightful place. That is exactly what secular education does.

It isn't enough, however, for me to simply assert that schooling is discipleship. I must also make an argument for supporting that assertion and do so from within a sound biblical framework. That is my goal in this chapter. So let's begin with this question: Does the Bible have anything to say about "schooling"? I believe it does—a lot, actually.

So, let's dive in and take a look at what we discover when we consider in God's Word how best to educate and equip our children for life in this broken world.

## Biblical Principle 1: The Goal of Christ-centered Schooling, As Is The Goal of Disciple Making, Is to Discover and Live Out the Mind of Christ in a Discerning, Disciplined, Devoted Way.

Let me state this as clearly and kindly as I can. The evangelical church has lost its mind. Ponder this observation by Harry Blamires:

> There is no longer a Christian mind. There is still, of course, a Christian ethic, a Christian practice, and a Christian spirituality. As a moral being, the modern Christian subscribes to a code other than

that of the non-Christian. As a member of the Church, he under-takes obligations and observations ignored by the non-Christian. As a spiritual being, in prayer and meditation, he strives to cultivate a dimension of life unexplored by the non-Christian. But as a thinking being, the modern Christian has succumbed to secularization. He accepts religion—its morality, its worship, its spiritual culture; but he rejects the religious view of life, the view which sets all earthly issues within the context of the eternal, the view which relates all human problems—social, political, cultural—to the doctrinal foun-dations of the Christian Faith, the view which sees all things here below in terms of God's supremacy and earth's transitoriness in terms of Heaven and Hell.[5]

Sadly, the problem was not new in 1963 when Balmires wrote his book, and it has only gotten worse. As Charles Malik, a former president of the United Nations, observed, "I must be frank with you: The greatest danger confronting American evan-gelical Christianity is the danger of antiintellectualism. The mind in its greatest and deepest reaches is not cared for enough."[6]

In responding to this painfully true observation, J. P. Moreland wrote, "This with-drawal and marginalization of the church has had devastating consequences for our attempt to produce vibrant, confident disciples and to penetrate our culture with a Christian worldview and the gospel of Christ."[7]

Now, consider that Moreland's observation was written nearly a quarter of a century ago and that over these intervening years there have been untold numbers of conferences on evangelism, church growth, worship, prayer, body life, and social justice—none of which has done much to slow, much less reverse, the decline of genuine biblical faith in the USA and in much of the world.

Yes, there are still millions of Americans attending church on a somewhat regular basis. And yes, there are some numerically growing churches. What's clearly missing, however, is a multiplying number of vibrant, confident disciples who are penetrating and influencing our culture with anything resembling a truly biblical life and world-view.

As a result, it has become increasingly difficult to do His work, His way. In fact, I've become increasingly confident that we don't actually understand the nature of the work to which we have been called. If we believe that our primary responsibility is to increase the size of the nursery, so to speak, then we will design a strategy to care for a growing number of infants. If we believe, however, that our task should focus more on preparing people for an invasion of a hostile world, then our strategies will look significantly different. So, what would such a strategy look like?

Permit me to begin with one of my most significant "aha" moments. I was a young teacher just a few years out of Bible college when I came across a book titled *On Being Human: The Nature of Spiritual Experience*, published by InterVarsity Press.[8] In that book the authors, Ranald Macaulay and Jerram Barrs, introduced me to a concept they called an "organizing principle." It completely changed how I view the world and my role in that world. They argued that a primary way to understand the purpose of life was to ponder the meaning of the following passage found in Genesis chapters 1 and 2:

> Then God said, 'Let us make man in our image, after our likeness. And let them have dominion over the fish of the sea and over the birds of heaven and over the livestock and over all the earth and over every creeping thing that creeps on the earth. So God created man in his own image, in the image of God he created him; male and female he created him. . . . The lord God took the man and put him in the garden of Eden to work it and keep it. (Genesis 1:26–27, 2:15)

I had grown up in a church tradition that informed me that my role in the world was basically twofold. First, I was to live a righteous life, meaning I was to avoid sin (including movie attendance, card playing, dancing, mixed bathing, and drinking, among other things); secondly, I was to share my faith with the intent to see others rescued from the consequences of their sinful state and behavior. It was a pretty simple way of looking at the world. It was also a flawed way of looking at the world.

Having said that, I am not suggesting that living righteously and sharing the gospel with people are bad things. On the contrary, those are good, essential things. Those things are not, however, a full, robust understanding of the role a follower of Jesus Christ is to play in this world.

As Macaulay and Barrs began to unpack what it means to be one made in the image of the immortal Creator God, my whole worldview shifted. As they observed, one made in the image of God bears a likeness to that image. While, for example, we are not omniscient, knowing all things, we do have the capacity to know things. We can ponder, and learn, and then act on what we know, which is quite unlike the rest of God's creation.

God is creative. As one created in His image, so am I. I can't, as God did, create something out of nothing, but I can create wonderful things, beautiful things, useful things, remarkable things like music and art. I can design. I can build. I can imagine something inside my head and bring it to life, so to speak.

God is also relational. As one created in His image, so am I. While our sin nature may make relationships a challenge, I can still pursue them and develop them and enjoy them. Indeed, it is difficult to live in this world without them.

God is strategic as well. As one created in His image, I must learn that simply reacting to events is not the best approach to life. I'm not stuck in a world where all I can do is respond to forces beyond my control. I can ask the question, "What if?" What if I did A instead of B? What if I chose a different course of action than what has previously been typical for me, or for the organization of which I am a part? What if I could combine A and B in a new way to create C?

And in the process of thinking through the implications of what I was reading, a whole new world opened to me.

A few years later this concept took on a greater depth as I was studying through John's Gospel. I was preparing a sermon from the seventeenth chapter, in which John records the prayer Jesus prays in the garden. I'd read through that text many times, but on this occasion a bit of grammar caught my attention. In verse 4 Jesus prays, "I glorified you on earth, having accomplished the work that you gave me to do." As I said, what caught my attention was the verb tense Jesus uses.

He doesn't say, "Father, I am about to bring You glory by what I am about to do." No, instead He says, "I have already glorified You; I have already accomplished the work that You gave me to do." As a good Baptist, I struggled for a bit here because I had always believed that the sum total of the work Jesus was given to do was the work of redemption. To fulfill that task, He had to first die by shedding His blood and then be brought back to life. At the moment of His prayer, however, He was still very much alive. So the question that came to mind was this: In what manner could Jesus say, "I have already fulfilled the purpose for which I was sent into the world"?

Now, most assuredly Jesus did come to provide a sacrifice sufficient to satisfy the just demands of a holy God. No one else could do what He was sent to do. There was more, however, to His mission here on planet Earth than His redemptive work on the cross. Redemption is not simply a matter of our personal eternal destiny. The goal of redemption is restoration. Through Christ's sacrifice we are being restored to our true purpose. Redemption and restoration are not, however, limited to individuals; it extends to the very fabric of creation.

How that redemption and restoration can best be extended to the world around us is hinted at in verse 6 when He says, "I have manifested your name to the people whom you gave me out of the world." So what does that mean? D. A. Carson provides some insight on that statement. "To these people, then, Jesus has revealed God's name . . . doubtless [summing] up all of Jesus' ministry, including the cross that lies just ahead. The revelation of God's name does not seem greatly different from the glorification of God on earth. God's name embodies his character; to reveal God's name is to make God's character known."[9]

In other words, we manifest God through our lives when we most clearly reflect the nature and character of God in how we live daily in this broken, fallen world. Our goal, therefore, is not just proclamation of the gospel; it is equally, and just as important, that we reflect the image of God to the world in as robust and accurate a manner as possible. Yes, God is love, and grace, and holy, and kind, and encouraging, and on goes the list of His character qualities. He is, however, also creative, and strategic, and wise, and thoughtful, and a defender of the weak, and on goes that list as well.

So, here's the point, here's what must be the heart of our disciple-making strategy. It is essential to instruct our kids about redemption. We must, however, also instruct them on how we can manifest the glory of God in every aspect of life under the sun. Our children and young people need to receive the kind of education that prepares them to fully and accurately reflect the full breadth of God's nature and character before a watching world. Anything less does a disservice to our children and brings discredit to our Lord.

## Partners together: parent, pastor, home, church. How can this work in the 21st century?

The focus of this chapter thus far has been on the reality that the 21st-century church, if it is to fulfill its mission to make disciples, must view that obligation from a much different perspective than what has been true for nearly two centuries now. The Great Commission is not simply about making converts. Rather, as I have noted, it is about instructing, equipping, and encouraging all who acknowledge Jesus as their Lord and

Savior for the work of ministry, for living lives aligned with both the teaching of Christ and the instruction of those who were called and inspired to author the books of the New Testament.

That is a huge task, one that requires us to employ all of our God-given resources in a wise and strategic manner. When I hear pastors say, "Schooling/discipleship is the responsibility of parents," my response is, "Of course parents bear responsibility for discipling their children." Who is responsible, however, for equipping parents for such a challenging role? Isn't that a primary role of the church? If so, why are so few resources invested toward that end?

A once-a-year parenting class just won't get it done. Periodic workshops are sadly insufficient for the enormity of the task. Parents are, without a doubt, as I will show in the next two chapters, given the primary responsibility to ensure that their children are "brought up in the discipline and instruction of the Lord."[10] They are also, without a doubt, doomed to failure without the assistance of capable partners.

The 21st century is simply too complex; the knowledge necessary for success in life is just too broad in scope, for any set of even the most dedicated parents to address on their own. This is where a healthy partnership between home, church, and schooling in its potentially various forms makes sense. In the next two chapters I am going to look more fully at that partnership. For now, I want to use a simple geometric design to illustrate my point.

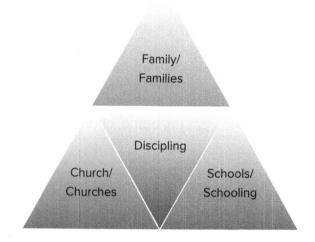

I have chosen a triangle for a simple reason. If you eliminate any of the three angles within a triangle, the entire thing falls apart; it collapses, utterly and completely. That is exactly what has happened over the course of the many decades since the founding of America's common school system in the 1840s. When the church and the family decided to outsource their most fundamental responsibility, we set off on a most dangerous journey, the consequences of which are now becoming unmistakable.

It's time—long past time, actually—to restore the integrity of this crucial triangle. How that can best be done is the focus of the following chapters.

## For Reflection

1. What has been your experience with disciple making in the churches that you have attended or led? How closely do those experiences align with the actual text of Matthew 28:18–20? How, in your mind, do the three elements of disciple making—evangelism, baptism, teaching to observe—work together toward the singular goal of making disciples?

2. As a parent, describe how you have been equipped to fulfill your responsibility to disciple your children. Have those efforts been sufficient? Helpful? If not, what would have been helpful?

3. Do you agree or disagree with the statement, "There is no longer a Christian mind"? Why do you believe that?

4. How does the idea of being made in the image of God impact how you think about your life and obligations as a follower of Jesus Christ?

Chapter 2

## It Is Possible—If

I opened the last chapter with a reference to the television and movie series *Mission Impossible*. If you've ever watched any of the old TV episodes or the more recent movies, you will soon note a few common themes. The first theme, unsurprisingly, is the seeming impossibility of all the missions. Having been a fan of the series for years, I find myself asking the same question over and over: "How are they ever going to accomplish this mission?"

A second theme, of course, is the overarching story line. First comes failure. Then comes reassessment and a somewhat different strategy. Third comes the eventual triumph, but not until the very last second and not before several near misses and heart-stopping action sequences. In the end, however, the good guys win.

There is, however, one key theme that nearly always unfolds at the beginning of each episode. That is when the leader of the IMF (Impossible Mission Force), be it Peter Graves in the old TV series or Tom Cruise in the recent movie series, puts together his team. As any leader knows, choose the wrong team members, and chances of success diminish significantly. Fortunately for both Peter and Tom, they choose wisely more often than not. When they make a bad choice or have a bad choice forced on them, however, there is always a price to be paid.

The same could be said about our choices for who should serve on the team we assemble to engage in the crucial job of making disciples of our children. Choose a good team and employ an effective strategy, and the chances of success increase dramatically. Choose poorly, either team members or strategy, and the possibility of success declines just as dramatically. That is a reality we can ill afford to ignore.

In my first chapter I tried to highlight the crucial role that the church must play in this drama. It was to the church that Jesus delivered the Great Commission. Thus, it is through the church that we are to fulfill that calling. The church, however, is not simply an organization. Rather, it is a body made up of redeemed people, all of whom are given gifts with the expectation that they will use those gifts to advance God's purposes in this world. Chief among those purposes is the call to make disciples.

In the following five chapters I will focus my attention on the members of that team and the strategies that should be employed in the mission of disciple making. Significant emphasis will be placed on the role of parents. They are not, however—indeed cannot be—the only members of the team for a simple, singular reason.

Permit me to explain it this way. The more you dilute something, the less potent it becomes. It's the difference between placing two grains of salt into a cup of water and adding two spoonfuls to that same cup of water. Modern life, which takes kids out of the home and into a complex array of influences, acts to dilute the crucial impact that a parent can have on the life and thinking of a child. It doesn't eliminate that influence, but it can, and often does, diminish that influence. So, what can a parent do in the context of today's reality?

## Biblical Principle 2: Remember That the Gift of a Christ-Centered Education Is a Parent's Obligation.

There's a big difference between the thoughtful advice of a friend who says, "Hey, you might consider" and a summons to appear in court. To one you might reply, "Thanks for the recommendation, but I think I'll pass." That same response probably wouldn't work in the other case. It's the difference between a suggestion and a mandate.

For example, when Paul writes to his young protégé Timothy, he often uses both kinds of language. In one case he suggests that it might do Timothy well to take a little wine for his stomach's sake. It is the kind of thing we do all of the time when talking to a friend with a health issue. I'm sure that you've heard that kind of advice and equally sure that you've given out that same kind of advice. My wife has been encouraging people to add barley green to their daily diet for years. Almost no one does. Her recommendation simply does not carry the force of law.

There are other times, however, when Paul's language is far more authoritative and directive. For example, in 2 Timothy 4:1 we read, "I solemnly charge you in the presence of God and Christ Jesus . . . preach the word." "Solemnly charge" translates a form of the verb *diamarturomai*, which carries the idea of giving a forceful order or directive. The apostle has twice before used the verb to admonish Timothy (1 Timothy 5:21; 2 Timothy 2:14). The aged warrior of the faith, whose godly life was totally committed to the service of Christ, again seeks to capture Timothy's undivided attention for what he is about to say."[1]

Because it is spoken as a directive by someone possessing the authority to do so, the recipient, in this case the young pastor Timothy, doesn't get to say, "Oh well, that just doesn't suit me. I think I'll go in a different direction." You either take the action indicated by the command, or you choose a course of disobedience.

In the military, the price for choosing to disobey an order is typically time in the brig. At your place of employment, it can cost you your job. If it's the IRS calling, well, you ignore that letter at your own peril. So, in addressing questions about disciple making it is crucial to determine whether the Scripture provides some thoughts to ponder or whether the Scripture makes a demand of us. To answer that question, I am going to plunge into an examination of one of the key texts on the matter of parents' responsibility as it relates to the schooling of their children.

## Parents, Don't Do This; Do This Instead

In the apostle Paul's letter to the church in Ephesus, we read what should be familiar words: "Children obey your parents in the Lord for this is right." Let me stop right there to ask you a question. Are those words given as a command or as a suggestion? I think most of you would say, "Well, that clearly sounds like a command." I think you would be right in making that observation.

Paul continues, "Honor your father and mother (for this is the first commandment with promise) that it may go well with you and that you may live long in the land." What do you think? Commandment or suggestion?

Next, Paul speaks to fathers and mothers: "Fathers, do not provoke your children to wrath but bring them up in the discipline and instruction of the Lord." So again, what do you think? Commandment or suggestion? I suspect all reading this book would agree. Paul isn't giving parents a suggestion here. He is issuing a mandate. We certainly would agree that provoking a child to wrath is wrong. I don't think there is much of an argument about that point. And I think we have a fairly good idea of what wrath is and what behavior on the part of a parent would produce that kind of response.

What about the second part of that directive, however? What does Paul mean when he uses the words, *"bring them up in the discipline and instruction of the Lord"*? It is in understanding the meaning of those words that we begin to get at the heart of finding an answer to this question: Is Christ-centered education a mandate or a maybe?

Let's begin with that phrase, *"bring them up."* The meaning is simple: Parents have the responsibility to provide for their children, and certainly this involves providing them with the basics of life—food, clothing, and shelter; but the phrase has a broader sense as well. Parents must also provide for the emotional and spiritual welfare of their children. They must seek to protect them from harm, and not just physical harm but all that would harm their heart and mind, that would threaten their well-being. By the way, did you know that the number one reason that parents choose to enroll their children in a Christ-centered school is safety? Interesting.

So here is an observation. The world we inhabit is a fascinating, wondrous place— so much beauty, so many intriguing places, so much to explore and know. As a parent, don't you want your children to have the opportunity to explore and experience all that God has given us in His majestic creation? I suspect so. I suspect, as well, that you are doing all within your ability to give that gift to your children, just as you should.

The world is, however, also a dangerous place. I don't think most of you would just hand your young children the keys to your car and say, "Here you go. Have fun." Your kids might want you to do just that, but you are too wise to give in to their immature desire. You understand that the possibility of disaster is just too great.

I spent my summers growing up on my granddad's ranch in the Hill Country of central Texas. During those summers I learned to do a lot of things, but high on my list of fun activities were riding and hunting. In both cases I was carefully shown how to act around horses and how to handle firearms. And I can tell you that whenever I violated the strict standards that both my grandfather and dad laid down for me, the consequences were immediate and severe.

I also remember my first solo deer-hunting experience. I knew I had achieved a certain level of independence because I had demonstrated that I understood how to act when in the field with a high-powered rifle and had learned as well how to respect the wildlife I was hunting. I had been brought up well. In a sense that's your job as a parent, and frankly, it is the job of pastors and churches as well.

To fully understand the whole phrase, however, we must dig more deeply into the next two words: discipline and instruction.

The word *discipline* is translated from the Greek word *paideia*. Paul uses that same word in 2 Timothy 3:16 when he reminds his young protégé that, "All scripture is breathed out by God and profitable for teaching [*paideia*], for reproof, for correction, and for training in righteousness, that the man of God may be complete, equipped for every good work" (1 Timothy 3:16).

Please forgive a bit of a side trip, but I think it's important to point out that Paul says, "All Scripture is breathed out by God and profitable." The all Scripture to which Paul would have been referring at that time in history was not just the emerging New Testament writings, but the full Old Testament as well. To suggest, as some have, that we can or must decouple the Old Testament from the New is a completely flawed and remarkably dangerous idea—one that, if adopted by the church, will have tragic consequences. This is not the time or place to dive deeply into why that concept must be rejected, but reject it we must if our goal is to equip people for every good work.

It is crucial to consider why Paul would use the word *paideia* in these instructions to parents in the church at Ephesus. Throughout his various letters to the churches of the Greco-Roman world, we observe that Paul is always careful, under the inspiration of the Holy Spirit, to use words that would resonate in the culture to which he is speaking. For example, when he communicates the redemptive work of Christ to the church in Rome, he doesn't have to spend a great deal of time explaining the meaning of the word redemption. Those people were well-acquainted with slavery. They understood redemption as an act that purchases a slave out of the marketplace and then sets that slave free. People who have never lived as slaves may miss the full implication of the meaning of redemption. Believe me, however, when I say that the people of ancient Rome got the meaning right away.

The same would be true of a word like *paideia*. It is not a word in common usage today, except in some education circles. It surprises me, however, that even quality Bible scholars don't always grasp the implications of its use in this text. I love, however, what John Piper has to say about *paideia*. He writes, "This word signifies the actions that a father takes to give his children the abilities and skills and character to live life to the glory of God." It "involves being shown how to do the things the Christ-exalting life requires and being held accountable to them as well as you can."[2]

He goes on to observe, "That is, a father will guide all his words and ways by God's Word and depend on God's wisdom (and remember that the fear of God is the place we begin to discover that wisdom) and strength to apply them and make everything serve the glory of God. In other words, the most important thing in raising children is that they come to see Christ, the Lord, as supremely valuable as Savior and Lord and Treasure of Life."[3]

Now try to imagine that happening at your local public school.

There is more to understanding *paideia*, however, and it is nearly always over-looked by even the most careful of biblical scholars. Remember, as I said, that Paul chooses his words with care as he seeks to communicate eternal truth in culturally relevant language. He does so because he rightly understands that people's understanding of things is often shaped by the cultural context in which they live. The use of the word *paideia* is an example of this.

So how would a citizen of Ephesus and a member of the church in that city have understood Paul's use of that word? What was meant by *paideia* in the Greco-Roman culture? Richard Tarnass helps provide an answer to those questions. *Paideia* was understood as, "The classical Greek system of education and training which came to include gymnastics, grammar, rhetoric, poetry, mathematics, geography, natural history, astronomy, and the physical sciences, history of society, and ethics and philosophy, *the complete pedagogical course of study necessary to produce a well-rounded, fully educated citizen*"[4] (my emphasis).

That the evangelical church of the 19th, 20th, and now the 21st centuries has for the most part not understood that reality is, as Mark Noll observed, a genuine scandal.[5] That we have so easily been able to separate all knowledge into two broad categories, the secular and the sacred, has done incalculable harm to the church and the culture in which we live. Sometimes I just want to cry, "Wake up!" Can't we see the damage being done by our actions? We think we are doing good by insisting that our kids be "salt and light" in the public schools. In reality we are doing far more to contribute to the decline of our culture and the weakening of the church than any good we think we may be accomplishing.

If there was any real hope of redeeming the public-school system as it currently functions in the USA, I would still think the same thing. Indeed, our job as parents and pastors is first and foremost the task of developing followers of Jesus Christ who are both fully devoted and fully discerning.

There are already many adults seeking to make a difference in the public-school arena. And on a one-by-one basis those adults do make a difference in the lives of a handful of kids. But let's be honest. On a larger scale their efforts, while heroic, haven't changed the overall direction of American public schooling. If the Christian teachers and educators and board members in public education haven't been able to turn the ship, I don't think that our children, who are ill-equipped for the task, are going to make any real difference.

If the church wants to make a positive impact in the lives of kids, I would suggest that they begin thinking about how they can make a quality Christ-centered education accessible to the tens of thousands of kids struggling to make sense of the world while attending the truly broken schools in our urban centers. It is the greatest mission field in the world, and it is right on our doorstep. Sadly, our response has been pretty feeble. We spend millions funding mission efforts all over the emerging world, but we ignore an area of great need right here. It's time that we figure out how to reach our own world. And please don't speak about a parent's responsibility as though that absolves us from reaching out to the "least of these." Sadly, 70% of children in urban African American communities live in single-parent homes. If parents in middle America can't do it alone, how can we expect those moms to do it alone?

I have an intimate understanding of that reality. My dad walked out on my mom, my brother, and me when I was in middle school. I know the anger and pain that comes with that abandonment. I know the difficulty a single mom faces in that situation. I know what it is like to try and figure out how to make financial ends meet at the end of the month. And I know that I would not be sitting here pounding away at my keyboard working on this book had it not been for a church—and school—that took seriously the job of discipling.

We, as the church, like the nation of Israel, have an obligation to those who are in the greatest need. Francis Schaeffer, that great theologian and prophet from the last decades of the 20th century, once remarked that God would hold America accountable for two great sins. The first sin was our long embrace of slavery and our consequent failure to address that sin even after shedding so much blood to abolish slavery. Is there anyone living in the USA today who doesn't see the price we are still paying for allowing that evil institution? The second sin flows directly from that first one. It is our lack of compassionate and wise use of our wealth. Maybe giving "the least of these" an opportunity to learn more of the Lord and how that knowledge can transform life would be a good place to start a better work.

Now back to that second word. The KJV gives us the word "admonition" or "instruction" as a translation for the Greek word *nouthesia*. Some of you might be familiar with the nouthetic counseling movement. Those who are part of that movement take direction from the word *nouthesia*, which literally means, "putting in mind." Paul uses this word in his letter to the church in Colossae when he writes, "Him we proclaim, warning everyone and teaching everyone with all wisdom, that we may present everyone mature in Christ" (Colossians 1:28).

As John Piper observes, "The idea of warning is prominent. One major Greek lexicon defines the word like this: 'to counsel about avoidance or cessation of an improper course of conduct [see 1 Thessalonians 5:14, I Corinthians 4:14, 2 Thessalonians 3:15]." Piper then goes on to make this key observation: "The responsibility is given primarily to parents but they are free to enlist help from others—indeed they are encouraged to do so."[6] Absolutely, because in all reality we can't do it alone.

This second word is crucial because as all of us know from personal experience, information alone is not enough. We all need people to come alongside us to encourage us, to pray for us, to challenge us, to hold us accountable, to sharpen our thinking. That again is why we need one another and need a healthy body. Have I said it enough times? We can't do it alone. And believe me, neither can your kids. And believe me on this as well: A couple of hours a week just won't get the job done. Not even close.

What Paul is saying to these parents is simple. There is a cultural *paideia* of which we must all be aware. There is, however, a distinctively Christian *paideia* that helps us understand

- How we can know what we know
- How we can know what we know about ourselves and the world in which we live
- How we can best act in light of what we know to be true truth
- How we can process that into a fully integrated life
- And here is the key: It is a process for which God holds parents, not the state, responsible.

The responsibility of parents and of the church working together is to find the best way to ensure that all children and young people are fully aware of both the cultural *paideia* and the Christian *paideia*. Without the ability to think through and apply both to the decisions all of us are required to make on a daily basis, and on the actions that all of us are required to take on a daily basis, we put our children at grave risk.

## Biblical Principle 3: The Guide for Christ-Centered Education Must Be a Servant of Christ.

Sometimes the simplest words have the most profound impact. Just spend a few minutes each day in reading through Psalms and Proverbs. Just a chapter a day. You don't have to dig deep every day, but I suspect that you will end up wanting to better understand the insights that lie behind such beautiful and evocative language.

Jesus frequently used similar kinds of imagery when He spoke. Think of the Sermon on the Mount. Think of His parables. Think of His many confrontations with the scribes and Pharisees. Here is one of our Lord's statements that caught my attention. Jesus asks a pretty simple question and then makes an equally profound observation. "Can a blind man lead a blind man? Will they not both fall into a pit? A disciple is not above his teacher, but everyone when he is fully trained will be like his teacher" (Luke 6:39–40).

That observation brings us to a crucial observation: We live in turbulent times, times from which we cannot disengage, times that require a wise guide. I don't think many of us would choose a blind person as our guide for a rafting trip down the raging Colorado River. It wouldn't matter whether that person was exceptionally bright, or caring, or hard-working, or committed to saving the environment. Blindness might not keep a person from doing a lot of things, but it would most likely disqualify him or her from acting as a river-rafting guide.

A lot of public-school teachers—in fact, the majority of them—possess the qualities I mentioned above. Plus, many of them are truly good at the art and science of instruction. Put simply, they are skilled, competent educators. Many of them, however, are spiritually blind, and at the end of the day they are pretty likely to lead their students into a ditch.

Even Christian teachers in public schools, while not personally blind, are handicapped by the curricular choices made by people whose worldview is certainly not consistent with the Scriptures. Those teachers may do all that is possible to limit the impact of that curriculum, but at the end of the day they are employees of a system that doesn't leave a lot of wiggle room for either content or instructional strategy. I applaud those Christian teachers in the public system who do all they can to be an in-carnation of Christ in a dark place, but I also know that such efforts are often thwarted by legal and cultural realities.

And, while I am a strong proponent of charter schools, at the end of the day they are still public schools and are limited as to what they can do to elevate Christ through the curriculum they may utilize. Depending on who serves as head of school and who serves on the school board, there may be a bit more flexibility for teachers. At the end of the day, however, the laws governing the public-school system in this country, laws that have long outlawed God, still apply to charter schools.

I know that a lot of churches are finding ways to work with charter schools and even local public schools. I certainly applaud those efforts. At the end of the day, however, it is still the blind leading the blind in the classroom, and there is little probability on the horizon of any meaningful change in public policy. If churches want to make a difference for kids, then it's time to step beyond current strategies and get serious about how to make Christ-centered education more accessible to a broader segment of the population. Half-measures won't get the job done. I will address this more fully in my final chapter.

## Godly Wisdom Instead

Let me begin this section with a simple definition: The fool is a person who has decided, "There is no God" (Psalm 14:1). Now it would be tempting to include in that definition only those who claim to be atheists. That would be a mistake. Many people claim to believe that God exists. Far fewer, however, would describe God in the same way as you probably do. Even fewer would be able to articulate what needs to be known of God and how what is known should shape how all of us are to live life in a fallen world. Fewer still have what we would call a well-developed biblical worldview.

One thing is certain, however, and the Scriptures make this quite clear. To systematically expose our children, our young people, or ourselves to the teaching and example of those the Bible identifies as fools is not simply discouraged by God, it is prohibited.

The book of Proverbs makes this clear in numerous places:

- "O simple ones, learn prudence; O fools, learn sense. Hear for I will speak noble things, and from my lips will come what is right, for my mouth will utter truth; wickedness is an abomination to my lips. All the words of my mouth are righteous; there is nothing twisted or crooked in them." (Proverbs 8:5–8)
- "Whoever walks with the wise becomes wise, but the companion of fools will suffer harm." (Proverbs 13:20)
- "A scoffer seeks wisdom in vain, but knowledge is easy for a man of understanding. Leave the presence of a fool, for there you do not meet words of knowledge." (Proverbs 14:6–7)
- "The tongue of the wise commends knowledge, but the mouths of fools pour out

folly." (Proverbs 15:2)

- "The lips of the wise spread knowledge; not so the hearts of fools." (Proverbs 15:7)
- "A scoffer does not like to be reproved; he will not go to the wise." (Proverbs 15:12)
- "The heart of him who has understanding seeks knowledge, but the mouths of fools feed on folly." (Proverbs 15:14)
- "The heart of the righteous ponders on how to answer but the mouth of the wicked pours out evil things." (Proverbs 15:28)
- "Whoever isolates himself seeks his own desire; he breaks out against all sound judgment. A fool takes no pleasure in understanding, but only in expressing his opinion. An intelligent heart acquires knowledge, and the ear of the wise seeks knowledge." (Proverbs 18: 1–2, 15)
- "Folly is bound up in the heart of a child, but the rod of discipline drives it far from him. Incline your ear and hear the words of the wise, and apply your heart to knowledge, for it will be pleasant if you keep them within you, if all of them are ready on your lips. That your trust may be in the Lord, I have made them known to you today, even to you." (Proverbs 22:15, 17–19)
- "By wisdom a house is built, and by understanding it is established; by knowledge the rooms are filled with all precious and pleasant riches. A wise man is full of strength, and a man of knowledge enhances his might, for by wise guidance you can wage your war, and in abundance of counselors there is victory." (Proverbs 24:3–6)
- "If a wise man has an argument with a fool, the fool only rages and laughs and there is no quiet." (Proverbs 29:9)

David speaks to this reality as well in Psalm 1, where he writes, "Blessed is the man who walks not in the counsel of the wicked, nor stands in the way of sinners, nor sits in the seat of scoffers; but his delight is in the law of the lord, and on his law he meditates day and night."[7]

If those words aren't enough to capture your attention and challenge your current view of how we should educate kingdom kids, then I hope that you might consider one additional observation from our Lord.

Matthew tells us of a moment in the ministry of Jesus when His disciples came to Him with an intriguing question, "Who is the greatest in the kingdom of heaven?" You may be familiar with what happens next. Jesus calls a child to stand next to Him and says the following: "Truly, I say to you, unless you turn and become like children, you will never enter the kingdom of heaven." In a less technologically advanced age we would say, "Lots of ink has been spilt" in attempting to explain what Jesus was actually saying with that comment.

I'd like to focus, however, on what comes next in that text. While continuing to answer the initial question, He says something that to anyone's ear would sound harsh: "Whoever receives one such child in my name receives me, but whoever causes one of these little ones who believe in me to sin, it would be better for him to have a great millstone fastened around his neck and to be drowned in the depth of the sea" (Matthew 18:1–6).

Wow! That's pretty severe language, by anyone's estimation. Imagine if that was said from any pulpit today. Imagine if by chance someone in the congregation recorded a video of that part of the sermon. Now imagine that video uploaded to the internet. How long do you think it would take before that pastor became a target of scorn? Can you hear the commentaries from the 24/7 news mob dripping with contempt for such an evil thought? I certainly can.

By the way, this is just one of many passages that give the lie to the picture of Jesus as just some meek and mild teacher who only went about imploring people to love one another. Sometimes He was anything but meek and mild. I'm pretty certain that "meek and mild" would not be the words used by the moneylenders to describe the man who kicked over their tables and ran them out of the temple courts. Nor do I believe that is the portrait the high priest, scribes, and Pharisees would paint of the man who described them as "nests of vipers" and "tombs filled with bleached bones."

Yes, Jesus was gentle when gentleness was called for. He was, however, also unsparing to those whose beliefs and behaviors caused harm to others. And no greater harm can be done than causing a little one to stumble in faith and, as a result, stumble in life. Please put this thought firmly in your mind: *Nothing is so harmful to a developing mind than systematic exposure to error.* It is in that kind of context that stumbling is most likely to occur. Yet that is exactly what happens daily in any educational environment that has declared, "No God!" Here is why.

The apostle Paul, writing to the leaders of the church at Ephesus, gives some clarity about a key purpose of the church when he writes, "And he gave the apostles, the prophets, the evangelists, the shepherds and teachers, to equip the saints for the work of ministry, for building up the body of Christ, until we all attain to the unity of faith and the knowledge of the Son of God, to mature manhood, to the measure of the stature of the fullness of Christ, so that we may no longer be children, tossed to and fro by the waves and carried about by every wind of doctrine, by human cunning, by craftiness in deceitful schemes."[8] Whew! That's quite a sentence and quite a task.

In his commentary on Paul's letter to the church in Ephesus, John MacArthur provides some insight on the language Paul employs in this text. Please give careful attention to what he has to say.

> Kubia (trickery) is the term from which we get cube, and was used of dice-playing. Just as today, the dice were often "loaded" or otherwise manipulated by professional gamblers to their own advantage. The term for dice therefore became synonymous with dishonest trickery of any sort. Craftiness is a similar term, carrying the idea of clever manipulation of error made to look like truth. Methodia (scheming) is used later in the letter to refer to the schemes of the devil. No doubt it has reference to planned, subtle, systematized error.

> It is spiritual children, such as were many of the Corinthian believers, who are in constant danger of falling prey to every new religious fad or novel interpretation of Scripture that comes along. Having no thorough knowledge of God's Word, they are tossed here and there by waves of popular sentiment and are carried about by every wind of new doctrine (or I might add of every new cultural fad) that seems appealing. Because they are not anchored in God's truth, they are subject to every sort of counterfeit truth—humanistic, cultic, pagan, demonic, or whatever. The New Testament is replete with warnings against this danger.[9]

James Boice adds this insight on what Paul is sharing here: "Children may be easily fooled. That is why parents have a special responsibility for the sound education and careful guidance of children."[10]

We forget sometimes just how vulnerable our children are, how easily they can be deceived and led astray, how quick they are to embrace flawed thinking for no other reason than that they haven't yet developed a robust way of evaluating what they hear in the classroom every day. We also forget that the world is filled with people who are willing and able to take advantage of immature minds and underdeveloped discernment.

Please don't misunderstand what I'm saying. I'm not suggesting that every teacher in the pubic system is seeking to undermine your kid's faith. We are naïve, however, if we don't recognize the reality that everyone speaks through a particular worldview perspective, and for most teachers in the public system that perspective is thoroughly secular in nature. Sadly, the same could be said of far too many Christians. We can be relatively orthodox in our theology but completely secular in our worldview.

We hear so much from professional educators that they are able to keep personal opinions and beliefs out of the classroom. That might have been the case a hundred years ago, and even then it was difficult to do. Today it is a virtual impossibility, especially when teachers often view their work the way a missionary would view theirs.

As Steven Garber notes, "The great tragedy is that in the twentieth century, laboring under the myth of neutrality, education in the West attempts to offer a value-free answer to the questions 'What is man?' and 'What is man for?' Not only is it philosophically and pedagogically impossible in terms of truthfulness about what is actually happening in education—but its fruit is Postman's [Neil Postman, *The End of Education*] technocrat's ideal: a person with no commitment and no point of view but with plenty of marketable skills."[11]

That is the grim truth about the current state of education in the USA, and no amount of wistful thinking will alter that reality. So, here are my questions. Parents, given Paul's clear instruction in his letter to the church at Ephesus, what must you do to ensure that your children are brought up in the *paideia* of Christ? Pastors, what responsibility do you bear as a shepherd, especially toward the most vulnerable in the flock over which you have been given responsibility? Are you allowing the wolves of false teaching to tear your flock apart, or are you standing in their way, saying with J. R. R. Tolkien's great character Gandalf, who when confronting the demon Balrog declares, "You shall not pass"?

Hard words, I know, but I think we have reached the place where tough talk is necessary. The time for timidity is past. It's time to put our best team in place—let me repeat, *our best team* in place—in our effort to fulfill the mission given us by our Lord Jesus Christ. No more half-measures. Remember: You can't do it alone. You can't.

So, where do we go from here? In the next chapter I am going to look more fully at the role of parents in the education of their children—a role that is crucial, especially in the context of our modern world.

## For Reflection

1. Considering the challenges inherent in the command to "Bring up your children in the *paideia* and *nouthsia* of Christ," what would be truly helpful to you as a parent? As a pastor? How does understanding the meaning of those two words impact how you think about the education of children?

2. Study Steven Garber's statement on the previous page. If what Garber says is accurate, how should that reality shape how you think about the education of your children and the education of the children who attend your church or school?

3. Ponder a bit on these questions and observations: Can a blind man lead a blind man? Will they not both fall into a pit? A disciple is not above his teacher, but everyone when fully trained will be like his teacher. Now ask yourself: How does that observation apply to your children and their education?

4. If Paul's instruction to parents in Ephesians 6:1–3 are commands and not suggestions, how should that reality impact your decisions about the education of your children?

Chapter 3

## It Is Required of a Steward

Who owns your child? You may never have given that question much thought. Others have, however. For example, in 1922 an initiative was adopted in the state of Oregon making it a crime for parents to enroll their children in any but a public school. Indeed, as the great constitutional attorney William Ball points out, "The state threatened to arrest all parents who would send their children to private schools."[1]

At the same time the state of Nebraska determined that, "children are to be common, and no parent is to know his own child nor any child his parent. . . . The proper officers will take offspring . . . into the pen or fold."[2] Stop and carefully ponder that language for a second. Fortunately, the Supreme Court of the United States, in one of its most consequential decisions, Pierce v The Society of Sisters, ruled that, "The child is not the mere creature of the state." Now carefully consider what the members of the court observed next: "Those who nurture him and direct his destiny have the right, coupled with the high duty to recognize and prepare him for additional obligations."[3]

Those are powerful and, if we allow them to be, convicting words. As a parent you have the right coupled with the high duty to direct the destiny of your child while preparing that child for his or her future life and obligations. In other words, this right to direct the education of your child comes with a huge responsibility. It isn't something to be taken lightly or something we simply outsource to complete strangers.

Sadly, the impulse of the state and other powerful interest groups to claim ownership of our children has not waned. That, I suppose, is to be expected. What troubles me more, however, is the apparent ease with which many, if not most, parents who identify as followers of Jesus Christ surrender the opportunity to fully shape their child's worldview to those who are increasingly hostile to that end.

Now let me be quick to add: Parents don't own their children any more than does the state. While parents are not owners, they are, however, stewards, with all of the obligations that come with that role. In the end, Christ is the owner. And while stewardship is not the same as ownership, it still obligates us to act wisely and responsibly regarding that over which we have been named a steward.

For example, as the apostle Peter reminds us, "each [of us] has received a gift" and we are therefore called to "use" that gift to "serve one another, as good stewards of God's varied grace."[4] We are to do this, Peter argues, "in order that in everything God may be glorified through Jesus Christ." So, while we may not be the owners of our children, we are stewards of them because as the psalmist reminds us, "Children are a gift of God."[5]

Hence a second question: What then is required of a steward? If children are a gift from God and if I am to steward that gift wisely, what then must characterize my stewardship? What actions must I pursue? What obligations must I undertake? And do I really understand that in the end it is the owner who will evaluate my stewardship efforts?

To answer that question, let me begin with some background on the word steward as it is used in the Scriptures. "The Greek (oikonomos) for steward literally means 'house manager,' a person placed in complete control of a household. The steward supervised the property, the fields and vineyards, the finances, the food, and the other servants on behalf of his master."[6]

That last phrase, "on behalf of his master," does not suit our 21st-century ear. In fact, I suspect that it offends the sensibilities of even those of us who identify ourselves as followers of Jesus Christ. Even more offensive is the idea that we are not only stewards but servants, literally slaves. Yet the apostle Paul proudly proclaims that lowly position for himself repeatedly in his many letters to the churches.

For example, in his letter to the church at Corinth he clearly states this reality when he writes, "Let a man regard us in this manner, as servants of Christ and stewards of the mysteries of God." To the church in Philippi he declares in his greeting, "Paul and Timothy, servants of Christ Jesus." Yes, Paul was an apostle. As such, he possessed all the authority granted to one in his position. Like Christ, however, he chose to set aside the privileges that came with that position to take on the life of a servant.[7] Paul understood and fully embraced his role and responsibility as steward and servant.

Culturally relevant or not, we must never forget that we, like Paul, are also both servants and stewards. We own nothing. Everything we possess belongs to and comes from Christ. Our responsibility, therefore, is to exercise wise stewardship on behalf of our Lord as we seek to advance His purposes in this world, and to fulfill those obligations in a manner that brings Him glory. The apostle Paul reminds us of that reality when he writes, "You are not your own. You are bought with a price. Therefore, glorify God."

So, what are the qualities and obligations of a steward that should impact how we think of and decide about the education of our children? Here are some thoughts that I hope you will ponder as you consider your responsibility as a steward of God's gracious gift. Every steward should exemplify the following qualities and obligations.

## The Good Steward Is Faithful and Trustworthy.

Faithfulness or trustworthiness is the first quality and obligation of a steward. In fact, according to the apostle Paul, it is a requirement.[8] This is important because the steward is "entrusted with his master's household and possessions; and without faithfulness he will ruin both."[9] That may sound pretty harsh until you consider the level of freedom that the master gives to the person serving as a steward.

In one sense that kind of freedom is akin to the self-determination that a wise school board affords a head of school. The effective board, like the wise owner, provides guidelines and even some limitations that must inform the decisions made and actions taken by a head of school. That flexibility can only be given, however, where there is a high degree of trust between the head and the board. That high level of trust is, however, only possible when the person given oversight acts faithfully with complete integrity.

When God gives you the gift of children, He is entrusting something of great value to you. You must never forget that; you must, therefore, act in a manner worthy of that trust.

## The Good Steward Is Humble.

The steward manages what belongs to another. The head of school, pastor of a church, or parent of children is not an owner, but a steward. And a steward must understand, "This does not belong to me." Living that way requires a high degree of humility.

Think of Moses, a prince of Egypt, who after a lavish life in the court of Pharaoh spends forty years in the Midian desert tending to flocks owned by his father-in-law. Think of John the Baptist, who proclaimed "he [Jesus] must increase, I must decrease." Think of Peter, who though an apostle, recognized that he did not own the flock for which he was called to "exercise oversight." Rather, he understands that he is simply a shepherd, working on behalf of the Chief Shepherd, who will one day return to claim his own.[10]

## The Good Steward Is Diligent and Accountable.

Here it would serve us well to pause and consider Christ's parable of the talents. In that story, the owner, who is about to begin a journey, calls his servants to a meeting during which he entrusts to them a particular responsibility related to his property. Upon his return, he once again calls a meeting of those same servants to settle accounts.

During that accounting, two of the servants demonstrate that they have been diligent by wisely investing the resources provided to them. As a result, their lord then expresses great pleasure at their efforts. The third servant, however, has not acted wisely, nor has he been particularly diligent. As a result, he earns a severe rebuke from his lord.[11]

If, as I previously noted, parents have been entrusted with a great gift, then it seems reasonable that those so blessed have an obligation to fulfill their Lord's purposes in the lives of those children. Failure to properly invest in that wonderful gift would, it seems, put us at risk of receiving the same kind of rebuke as the unfaithful steward.

Here again is a concept that doesn't seem to fit well with our 21st-century American ethos. We really don't like the idea of accountability. We tend to view ourselves as essentially autonomous, owing allegiance to no one, held accountable by no one, responsible only to ourselves. This me-first attitude has led to terrible consequences, not only in our culture but within our churches as well.

I spend much of my time working with school leaders and board members in helping them think through how they can continue to excel while delivering the mission to which they have been called. There are many variables from one school to another. There are, however, also many constants. Schools that fail in their planning efforts are most often those who do not work diligently nor practice appropriate accountability. Schools that succeed most often do work diligently and are willing to appropriately hold one another accountable.

The idea of appropriate accountability is, by the way, one of the primary benefits of quality Christlike schooling. Developing a strong partnership with people who share your worldview and values makes sense, as does asking great teachers to come alongside parents to assist in fulfilling their stewardship responsibilities. That partnership is only possible, however, when you do share those common beliefs with that teacher. As the prophet said, "How can two walk together unless they be agreed?"[12]

A final thought on this point: We will give an account of our efforts. At some time, our Lord will require of us an explanation for how we have pursued our stewardship responsibilities as parents. We can't determine how our children will respond to our efforts. We can, however, determine the manner in which our children will be guided and supported as they wrestle with crucial questions about their purpose and place in this world. As a good steward, you simply can't leave that to "chance."

## The Good Steward Works to Make Things Better.

The first thing God does after He creates Adam is to give him a job: Manage My creation; steward My gifts to you. There are no directives telling Adam how to accomplish his task, and there is a single restriction: Don't eat the fruit off of a particular tree. Adam is given a huge amount of freedom. Sadly, he fails to obey that single decree.

The consequences of that failure have been catastrophic. Death enters the world, as does frustration, as our every effort is thwarted by thorns and thistles; drought and storm; selfishness, sloth, and foolish decisions. As Paul notes, because of that fall "the creation was subjected to futility" and continues to groan to this day.[13]

Now here's the good news. We have been given great gifts as the children of God. Among those gifts is the capacity to make better the world in which we live. Yes, the creation groans. Yes, human cultures often seem to be imploding. Yes, nations rise against nations. Yes, one group of people often harbors ill will toward another group of people. Yes, sometimes the world looks dark and dangerous. But here's the true reality amid all of that angst and anger: In all things we are more than conquerors through Him who loved us.[14]

We have been given the great privilege, opportunity, resources, and capacity through God's grace to make a profound difference in this broken world. We can, if we choose to do so, make things better. It's what stewards do. This truth must be passed on to our children. As part of our discipling responsibility, we've got to help our children and young people understand and embrace that truth while learning to act wisely and well as stewards of God's grace. Christian schooling done well will provide enormous help in fulfilling that responsibility.

There is more, however, to our responsibility as parents in the discipling of our children. We are not just to be stewards. We must also be shepherds.

## Shepherding Your Child's Heart

Have you ever wondered why we refer to pastors as shepherds? In actuality the word *pastor* simply means "shepherd." Pastors are by definition shepherds. That concept, however, like the word *steward*, or the word *slave*, is also a bit out of sync with our 21st-century sensibilities. We prefer words like leader, or coach, or encourager—all good words, but words that don't really capture what a shepherd does.

My grandfather raised sheep and goats in the Hill Country of Texas. That doesn't make me an expert on shepherding, but after spending most of my summers as a kid on his ranch, I do have a bit of perspective on how challenging a task shepherding can be.[15] Sheep are unlike most other domestic animals. They require a much greater level of attention than, say, cattle or goats, who are much more able to care for themselves.

Thus, I find it interesting that Jesus often compares people to sheep.[16] I think most of us would say, "I'm not at all like a sheep. I've done a pretty good job of figuring out the world in which I live and getting from point A to point B on my own." If you stop and think about that statement for just a minute, I think you'd have to acknowledge that in reality you got from point A to point B with a lot of guidance—shepherding, if you will.

Now I think we can all acknowledge that there are good guides and bad guides, quality guidance and flawed guidance. The author of Proverbs makes that clear when he writes, "Know well the condition of your flocks, and give attention to your herds."[17]

Again, if we stop for just a second to consider our early years, I suspect that most of us would be forced to admit that we are where we are today, that we are who we are today, that we can do what we do today, to a large extent because someone cared enough for us to ensure that we were fed, clothed, educated, and cared for in times of crisis. Leave a newborn lying in the snow without adequate clothing or food and the likelihood of survival is pretty low.

Thus, I believe that the concept of shepherding is an appropriate way to look at our responsibility as parents. In fact, I believe that shepherding, like stewardship, is an obligation given us by our Lord. As Paul Tripp puts it, "The parent is the child's guide. The shepherding process helps a child to understand himself and the world in which he lives. The parent shepherds the child to understand not just the 'what' of the child's actions, but also the 'why.' As the shepherd you want to help your child understand himself as a creature made by and for God."[18]

And here Tripp makes a crucial observation. "You cannot show him these things merely by instruction; you must lead him on a path of discovery. You must shepherd his thoughts, helping him to learn discernment and wisdom. This shepherding process is a richer interaction than telling your child what to do and think. It involves investing your life in your child in open and honest communication that unfolds the meaning and purpose of life. It is not simply direction, but direction in which there is self-disclosure and sharing. Values and spiritual vitality are not simply taught, but caught."

He then concludes with this final thought: "Proverbs 13:20 says, 'He who walks with the wise becomes wise.' As a wise parent your objective is not simply to discuss, but to demonstrate the freshness and vitality of life lived in integrity toward God and your family. Parenting is shepherding the hearts of your children in the ways of God's wisdom."[19] Parenting also requires, however, that those who stand in your stead (teachers for example) will provide the same kind of guidance that you provide. No wise shepherd turns the care of his sheep over to wolves.

Permit me four additional thoughts on the crucial shepherding role that is part of every parent's responsibility.

## Shepherding Is Highly Personal.

I won't reproduce the entire text here, but I would encourage you to read and ponder John 10. I will, however, highlight one portion of that text: "The sheep hear his voice, and he calls his own sheep by name and leads them out."[20] The shepherd, as revealed here, is certainly familiar with the sheep and the sheep with the shepherd. As David so memorably puts it, "The LORD is my shepherd."

If the research is accurate that the average father spends a mere fifteen minutes a day in face-to-face conversation with his children, then in what way can that father be shepherding his children? One of the most pernicious ideas that has gained currency today is the idea that quality time is more important than quantity of time. If, as Paul Tripp has observed, "This shepherding process is a richer interaction than telling your child what to do and think. It involves investing your life in your child," then we've got to disabuse ourselves of the unhealthy distinction between quality and quantity time. It is both.

I understand how challenging doing this can be in our current moment of time and history. Given all of our real obligations between work, home, and church, the task of spending quantity time that has a quality feel to it with our children can seem difficult if not impossible. If you want to truly shepherd your child's heart, however, you've got to find a way. Finding others to assist you in that shepherding responsibility certainly makes sense.

## Shepherds Are Relentless in Protecting Their Sheep.

I love David's response when turning down Saul's offer of armor for the upcoming battle with Goliath. "Your servant used to keep sheep for his father. And when there came a lion, or a bear, and took a lamb from the flock, I went after him and struck him and delivered it out of his mouth. And if he arose against me, I caught him by his beard and struck him and killed him. Your servant has stuck down both lions and bears, and this uncircumcised Philistine shall be like one of them, for he has defied the armies of the living God."[21]

Is that your posture toward your children? Will you put your own life at risk to protect them from harm? I suspect that you would respond to that question with a resounding yes! But here I am not just talking about the bully at the bike rack. I'm talking about the far greater harm that your children face every day from what they hear in the classroom at their local public school. So, another question: Do you truly see the danger your children face every day from what they hear and see in the classroom?

The apostle Paul doesn't sugarcoat that kind of danger when addressing the elders of the church in Ephesus. To them he says, "Pay careful attention to yourselves and to all the flock, in which the Holy Spirit has made you overseers, to care for the church of God, which he obtained with his own blood. I know that after my departure fierce wolves will come in among you, not sparing the flock."[22]

That is a pretty graphic image. I am certain that many of those serving in the church at Ephesus had seen the terrible carnage that could be inflicted on defenseless sheep by those fierce wolves. They certainly could understand the danger to themselves in taking on those predators. Paul, however, makes it clear that as shepherds it is their job to protect the flock. And make no mistake: As a parent that is your responsibility as well.

It puzzles me, however, that for the most part we don't seem to fully grasp the full extent of that responsibility. I could give illustration after illustration of how changes in the curriculum of state-funded public education puts children at risk.[23] I'll provide just one.

The state of California just recently (2019) amended its law on School Health Education, AB-329, which now forces discussions of transgender and LGBT material into the curriculum. Those changes include discussions on the use of lubricants, sex toys, and anal sex. Beyond that I will not go. I will note, however, that the law makes it virtually impossible for a parent to request an opt out for their children.[24] Sadly that is but one of many illustrations of how public schooling is being employed to shape how children see the world.

Now, given the corrupt culture in which we now live, wouldn't it make sense to discuss those issues? The answer is certainly yes. Who, however, do you want leading those conversations? What should be the foundation for those conversations? When should those conversations begin? Now, how do you think the advocates of such a curriculum would answer those questions?

As a parent-shepherd, your responsibility is to protect your children from those kinds of grievous wolves. Yes, you could run for the school board and seek to modify those kinds of outrageous actions and decisions. Given the foundation from which most secular educational practitioners operate, however, you will never be able to keep up. So, why not invest your resources in doing something that truly makes a difference in the lives of your children?

Do Christians have a role to play in America's secular public-school system? Yes, I think we do, and I'll address that in a later chapter. I just don't believe that putting our children at risk is the way to do that.

## Shepherds Are Equally Relentless in Providing Necessary Nourishment for Their Sheep.

I love what David says about his shepherd: With the Lord as my shepherd I shall not want. He makes me lie down in green pastures. He leads me beside still waters.[25] Note the phrase, "makes me lie down." Chuck Swindoll makes this observation about that phrase:

> I am told that sheep, being stupid animals, frequently are alarmed and actually run over each other, racing away from something that startles them. Their shepherd corrects the problem by catching a sheep and gently, yet firmly forcing it to lie down and feed quietly on the grass beneath its feet.[26]

I suspect that you may be thinking, "I'm not sure that I'm as stupid as a bleating sheep." I suspect you would be correct. I would, however, note two things. First, David seems to be referring to himself in this text. Pay careful attention to the language here: "He makes me lie down." David is clearly remembering a time when he needed the Shepherd to gently take hold of him and lead him to his necessary nourishment. Do you think we are really any different from David? Haven't you ever found yourself out of control, needing the gentle hand of Christ, our Shepherd? I know I have.

Secondly, if you and I need that kind of guidance on occasion, isn't it possible that our children would need similar guidance as well? In fact, given their lack of experience and immaturity, wouldn't the need for proactive guidance be a bit greater? Consider, for example, this statement from the book of Proverbs: "Foolishness is bound up in the heart of a child. The rod of correction will drive it far from him."

Wow! Is there a concept more out of sync with 21st-century thinking than a rod of correction? I suspect that such a word conjures up images of the cruel schoolmaster repeatedly striking a supposedly misbehaving student. Yet David tells us something very different about the rod when he writes, "Even though I walk through the valley of the shadow of death, I will fear no evil, for you are with me; your rod and your staff they comfort me."[27]

How do we reconcile those two images? First of all, we would need to understand how a shepherd used those two instruments, the rod and the staff. The rod was typically a short wooden club used to fend off predators. The shepherd's staff or crook was used for "prying a sheep lose from a thicket, brushing branches aside along a narrow path, and pulling wandering sheep out of holes into which they had fallen. He also used it to beat down high grass to drive out snakes and wild beasts. Like the rod, the staff was a symbol of the shepherd's power and strength."[28]

The rod and the staff were not weapons to be used against the sheep but as tools to protect them as they made their way to a place of nourishment and rest. Sometimes, however, while on that journey a sheep would head off in a dangerous direction. When that happened the shepherd's staff was used to return them to a safe path, and sometimes while using that staff the shepherd inflicted pain—not out of anger but out of necessity.

The rod and its usage, however, must be carefully understood and properly employed if it is to have a positive impact. "The book [of Proverbs] tacitly condemns the martinet; rather it teaches that the parents' chief resource is constructive, namely their 'law' taught with loving persistence. . . . This law is a wide term which includes commands but is not confined to them: basically it means direction, and its aim is to foster wise habits of thought and action which, so far from enslaving a person, will equip him to find his way through life with sureness and honor."[29]

This topic requires far more discussion than I can give it in this brief space. There are two things, however, that I'd encourage you as a parent to consider. First of all, as the above quote from Derek Kidner implies, using the rod appropriately requires patience, persistence, and intentionality. Secondly, using the rod in that manner is not optional if you hope "to foster wise habits of thought and action" and equip your child "to find his way through life with sureness and honor."

## Shepherds, Like Stewards, Remember What's Most Important.

History is filled with events we have been asked to remember. Independence Day is an example. On that day we remember the signing of a declaration calling for our independence from England. Memorial Day and Veterans Day are other examples. On those days we are asked to remember the sacrifices of those who have paid a painful price to secure our freedom as Americans. Phrases like, "Remember the Alamo" or "Remember Pearl Harbor" or "Never Forget" when spoken of the Holocaust are used as rallying cries in desperate times.

We are often asked to remember for two reasons. First of all, as time passes, we tend to forget even important events. Have you ever forgotten your spouse's birthday or even your wedding anniversary? Be honest. Our family calendar at home is marked with all the dates that we need to remember for a simple reason. We all tend to forget.

The second reason is akin to the first. When we forget, so will our children. When they forget, a new narrative is likely to emerge in place of the old, and what matters most can be lost to succeeding generations. The consequences of that forgetting can be painful, even devastating, for generations.

Joshua was clearly concerned with that possibility. That is why, when nearing death, he calls together the twelve tribes of Israel and delivers a powerful address in which he recalls all that Yahweh had done in bringing them to the land of promise.[30] In doing this, Joshua was simply repeating what Moses had done earlier as the people of Israel were poised to enter the land of promise.

In one of the most powerful passages in all of the Scripture, Moses, through the inspiration of the Holy Spirit, challenges the people of Israel with these words:

Now this is the commandment—the statutes and the rules—that the LORD your God commanded me to teach you, that you may do them in the land to which you are going over, to possess it, that you may fear the lord your God, you and your son and your son's son, by keeping all statutes and his commandments, which I command you, all the days of your life, and that your days may be long.

Hear therefore, O Israel, and be careful to do them, that it may go well with you, and that you may multiply greatly, as the Lord, the God of your fathers, has promised you, in a land flowing with milk and honey.

Hear, O Israel: The LORD our God, the LORD is one. You shall love the Lord your God with all your heart and with all your soul and with all your might. And these words that I command you today shall be on your heart. You shall teach them diligently to your children, and shall talk of them when you sit in your house, and when you walk by the way, and when you lie down, and when you rise. You shall bind them as a sign on your hand, and they shall be as frontlets between your eyes. You shall write them on the doorposts of your house and on your gates. (Deuteronomy 6:1–9)

Embedded in that presentation is something of crucial importance. Remembering requires immersion. God is not suggesting that periodic reflection on matters of importance will be sufficient to ensure that the torch of truth gets passed from one generation to another. If truth is to take root in the hearts and minds of a people, it must be continually recalled and diligently cultivated daily.

Now ask yourself this question: Is that how we are passing on truth in our world today? Be honest.

## It Does Take a Village; You Can't Do It Alone.

When Arnold Palmer, the iconic and gifted golfer, died a few years ago, there were many articles published and innumerable commentaries broadcast celebrating his life and accomplishments on and off the golf course. In virtually all of them, one thing was repeatedly observed. Arnold Palmer was not only an exceptional golfer; he was a genuinely good man. Story after story was shared by hundreds of people describing how this man who played golf with some of the most powerful people in the world always treated the common person with the same grace.

Arnold Palmer was not a saint. He was, however, a man who lived his life by a clear set of values that were forged, as he repeatedly noted, through a powerful relationship with his parents, Deke and Doris Palmer.

I love how Palmer described that relationship in a brief biography written near the end of his life. "I began my journey through this golfing life with Pap's unswerving guidance as the bedrock of just about everything I tried to do and how I chose to do it. My whole being has been a reflection of him. I wanted to emulate him, I wanted to be as tough as he was, and I wanted to do the things he did in the right way, as he did them."[31] I suspect that any of us would be thrilled to hear our children say something similar about us.

What really caught my attention, however, was how Deke Palmer managed to have such a powerful influence on his son. Lots of dads love their kids. Lots of dads have admirable qualities that they hope to pass on to their children. Lots of dads want to see their kids succeed in that quest. I'm not sure, however, that many dads today understand what it takes to succeed in that quest.

In fact, I'm fairly certain they miss an ingredient that is key to that process. So what is that ingredient? It's time—lots and lots of time spent together—during which we get to model and encourage crucial virtues and essential truths like integrity, respect, and a love for Christ and the Scriptures. There is simply no substitute for time. The quality-versus-quantity argument regarding time is, as I noted earlier, bogus. It must be both quality and quantity if we hope to have the kind of life-changing impact on our children that we say we desire.

Here's how Palmer described his dad's influence: "I practically grew up at my father's side. When my sister Lois Jean came along two years after me, Pap would take me with him to work so that my mom could keep a handle on my sister and things at home. Therefore—and here is the key point—I was around my father all day every day. There was really no way my immersion [please pay careful attention to that word] in Pap's environment wasn't going to have a huge influence on me."[32]

That description of Palmer's daily relationship with his father, by the way, sounds a lot like what Moses instructed the people of Israel to do as they prepared to go into the land of promise.[33]

Let me anticipate your response. "Alan, we no longer live in the kind of world into which Arnold Palmer was born. We just can't spend that kind of time with our kids. For us it's off to work every day, and the idea that our kids could tag along with us is just not reality."

I wouldn't disagree. That doesn't change the fact, however, that *someone every day* is shaping how your kids see the world. *Someone every day* is modeling values that will impact how your kids will act in the world. More importantly, someone every day is either pointing your child to Christ or distorting His image. Every day. Day in and day out. So, since you can't be there, who do you want filling in for you? In what kind of world do you want your child immersed?

It isn't that you as a parent don't have an impact on your kids. That impact, however, is becoming ever more limited by the realities of life in our current culture. It isn't that the church you attend can't have an impact on your kids. Reality, and research, tell us, however, that the two to three hours your child spends at church in a week and the few hours they spend in close contact with you each week are rather meager when compared with the hours they spend every day interacting with media or with the thirty-five hours a week they spend in school.

It's painful to acknowledge, but the people who operate Google, Facebook, Instagram, SnapChat, YouTube, and whatever new social media platform is coming down the pike, along with all of those who teach and coach your kids day in and day out, are in many ways having a greater impact in shaping reality for your child than you do.

And even good kids struggle. In his groundbreaking research on the religious and spiritual lives of American teenagers and young adults, Dr. Christian Smith of Notre Dame University concluded that, "The cultural ocean in which American adolescents swim saturates them in the ethos of therapeutic individualism. Therapeutic individualism defines the individual as the source and standard of authentic moral knowledge and authority, and individual self-fulfillment as the preoccupying purpose of life. Subjective, personal experience is the touchstone of all that is authentic, right, and true."[34]

As a result, God gets reduced to either a moral scold or a being whose existence has a singular purpose: Make my life better. There is virtually no sense of a transcendent God who has created us on purpose for a purpose and has called us to a life of holiness.

So, how can we, as parents and pastors, be assured that the virtues, values, and beliefs revealed in God's Word take firm root in the hearts, minds, and actions of our children and young people? There is no single simple answer to that question. What I do know, however, is that our children and young people are more likely to reflect the world in which they are immersed. Sadly, for some reason, in spite of the mounting evidence that we are losing an entire generation of our young people, that simple reality seems to elude the vast majority of Christian parents and pastors.

The point, and one that I will repeatedly sound, is this: We can't do our job of stewarding or shepherding alone. We need help. You need help. Children and adults need tons of encouragement. And I can tell you this with absolute confidence: No one will find the kind of encouragement envisioned in the Scriptures via social media. In fact, the opposite is true.

Our kids need to be immersed in a community of faith and learning where the efforts of parents and pastors will be multiplied and magnified. It does take a village, a community. You just need to ensure that it is the right village—a place in which people share your values, reinforce your worldview, care deeply for your children, and will join together with you in your stewarding and shepherding efforts.

So, here's my question: Do you really believe that will happen at your local state-funded, secular public school? If you believe so, then by all means make that choice. If not, however, what then?

It is crucial to remember, however, that as a parent who identifies as a follower of Jesus Christ, you have no greater responsibility than to ensure that your children become fully devoted and fully discerning disciples of our Lord. Consider David as an illustration of your stewardship and shepherding responsibility. As you may recall, David was the youngest of eight brothers, three of whom were serving King Saul on the front lines of a war between the Philistines and the nation of Israel. David's role during that time was to take provisions from home to his brothers.

If you read the account of that fearsome moment found in 1 Samuel 17, you will come across an interesting statement: "David rose early in the morning and left the sheep with a keeper and took the provisions and went, as Jesse had commanded him."[35] I hope you picked up on a key observation in that brief passage. David had a responsibility to carry food to his brothers, but he also had a responsibility to care for his father's flock. Since he, like most parents, couldn't be in two places at once, what did he do?

What he didn't do was shirk his responsibility. He didn't just take off for the front lines and leave his father's flock without oversight and protection. No, he did not.

According to the text, "he left the sheep with a keeper," someone who could stand in for him in his absence, someone whom David clearly trusted to fulfill the important responsibility of both steward and shepherd.

As I have already observed, every day that you send your child off to school, that is exactly what you do: You outsource the oversight, protection, and preparation of your children to someone—every day. So, it seems to me that every parent has a crucial question that must be asked and answered: To whom will I outsource the discipling of my children? *They are being discipled every day*—every day. Whom have you tasked with that responsibility?

An increasing number of parents have answered that question by choosing to homeschool their children. For many parents, however, homeschooling isn't an option. That reality doesn't, however, alleviate those parents from making an appropriately biblical decision regarding the education of their children.

In the next chapters it will be my goal to help describe the kind of person, the kind of place, and the kind of process most likely to provide the kind of help you need to fulfill your calling as steward and shepherd of your children.

## For Reflection

1. As a parent, pastor, or teacher, how should knowing your roles as both steward and shepherd of the children entrusted to your care impact your behavior and responsibilities, especially as it relates to the education of those children? Use the descriptions of a steward and shepherd in this chapter to help you in answering that question.

2. If you can't fulfill your role as steward and shepherd alone, or shouldn't fulfill those roles alone, how do you go about finding help?

3. Ponder this statement: "I was around my father all day, every day. There was really no way my immersion in Pap's environment wasn't going to have a huge influence on me." Now consider how that concept of "immersion" might impact decisions about how to educate your children.

Chapter 4

## The Why Behind the What

In answering that question, I am reminded of a scene from the movie *Indiana Jones and the Last Crusade*. In that movie, Indiana Jones and his father are searching for the fabled cup of Christ. In spite of personal betrayal and opposition from those nasty Nazis, they find the location far out in the desert. There is just one problem: There is more than one cup from which to choose. Indeed, there are dozens, and a choice must be made. Drink from the wrong cup, however, and you die.

And that is just what happens. The bad guy chooses a cup made of gold and covered with jewels because, as he notes, "This is the cup of a king." Of course, it is the wrong decision. And of course, he pays for that poor choice with his life—shown in a most gruesome fashion by filmmaker Steven Spielberg.

Indiana Jones, however, chooses a much simpler design, one that he believes would have been at home on the table of a carpenter. As the keeper of the cup declares, Indiana had chosen wisely. With that choice came life.

Most of us probably view such a story as nothing more than a rousing tale of derring-do and good versus evil, much in the same way as we would view the contemporary Marvel action movies. And for the most part I think that would make sense. Yet contained in that brief scene is a deep truth that it would do us good to ponder for just a moment. It is that truth I want to explore a bit in this chapter.

## A Foundational Presupposition

What drove the bad guy to make the choice he did? What do you believe shaped his thinking? Fortunately, we really don't have to speculate much to find an answer to that question because, in his own words, he gives us the key to his decision. In his mind Jesus was a king, and kings, after all, are accustomed to nothing but the best. Thus, the choice was easy; it just had to be the most elaborate and ornate of the cups on the table. Indiana Jones too was driven by his presuppositions. But he looked at Jesus through a very different lens. What he saw was a simple carpenter. Thus, his choice reflected that view. All of us make decisions in pretty much the same manner. We choose what most precisely reflects our view of the world. That view, directly or indirectly, impacts most of our choices, including those relating to the education of our children.

In an essay entitled "What Is Man?" T. S. Eliot speaks directly to this issue.

> We can have no clear or useful idea of what education is, unless we have some notion of what this training is for. Thus we come to inquire what is the purpose of education, and here we get deeply into the area of conflict.... The moment we ask about the purpose of anything, we may be involving ourselves in asking about the purpose of everything. If we define education, we are led to ask, "What is man?"; and if we define the purpose of education we are committed to the question "What is man for?" Every definition of the purpose of education, therefore, implies some concealed, or rather implicit philosophy or theology. In choosing one definition rather than another we are attracted to the one because it fits in better with our answer to the question, "What is man for?"[1]

His point is simple. We can only decide how best to educate our children when we have determined to what end their education must aim; in other words, we must identify the *why* behind the *what*. I have become convinced that until we can answer that question, we can never make a wise choice about how to educate and thus disciple our children.

So just what is the point of education? What is the why behind the what? As you can imagine, lots of thoughtful people have given an answer to that question.

- Socrates would tell us, for example, that the purpose of education is to produce "good men who act nobly."
- In similar fashion Dwight Eisenhower believed that "the true purpose of education is to prepare young men and women for effective citizenship in a free form of government."
- Anthony Burgess observed, "The purpose of education is to fit us for life in a civilized community, and it seems to follow from the subjects we study that the two most important things in a civilized life are Art and Science."

- According to Samuel Johnson, "The supreme end of education is expert discernment in all things—the power to tell the good from the bad and the genuine from the counterfeit."
- Martin Luther King observed something similar: "Education must enable one to sift and weigh evidence, to discern true from false, the real from the unreal, and the facts from fiction."
- Sydney J. Harris declared, "Most people are mirrors, reflecting the moods and emotions of the times; few are windows, bringing light to bear on the dark corners where troubles fester. The whole purpose of education is to turn mirrors into windows."
- "Education is," according to G. K. Chesterton, "simply the soul of society as it passes from one generation to the other."
- Justin Saldana said, "The purpose of schooling is the transmission of culture, the process by which the culture of a society is passed on to its children."[2]
- Steven Garber suggests that the goal many parents have for their children is to hand them what he calls the "passport to privilege," that we want them to pursue an education that focuses primarily at preparing them for a good job. Such an education tends to be very utilitarian, seeking to provide students not with life skills but with job skills.[3]

For many people today the transmission of current cultural norms has become the most prominent purpose of schooling in the USA. For those folks (often people who live within either the political class or educational establishment), the end toward which we should strive in education is helping a student better embrace current cultural norms, norms that unfortunately are often in conflict with those we find in Scripture. In our time those norms would revolve around questions of gender identity, social justice, "saving the environment," financial inequality, and a host of other issues that would require a radical reordering of how we view the world and our place in that world.

You don't have to be an afficionado of the twenty-four-hour news cycle to know that we are in the midst of an enormous cultural shift, one that Peggy Noonan, a writer for the *Wall Street Journal*, captured well in her July 27, 2019, column. In that column she takes a look at the role higher education is pursing while attempting to supercharge that shift. She compares what is happening today to what happened during the French

Revolution, a bloody and horrific time, and draws some uncomfortable parallels to what is taking place today. She writes,

> It was a revolution largely run by sociopaths. One, Robespierre, the "messianic schoolmaster," saw it as an opportunity for the moral instruction of the nation. Everything would be politicized, no part of the citizen's life left untouched. As a man was governed by an "empire of images," in the words of a Jacobin intellectual, the new regime would provide new images to shape new thoughts. There would be pageants and new names for things. They would change time itself.
>
> . . . it should be said that there is an aspect of self-infatuation, of arrogance, in telling people they must re-order the common language to suit [one's] own ideological preferences. There is a tone of, "I'm your moral teacher. Because you are incapable of sensitivity I will help you, dumb farmer. I will start with the language you speak."
>
> It's all insane. All of it. You wonder how the people who push all of this got so much power. But then, how did Robespierre?" [4]

I have included this piece for two simple reasons. First of all, Noonan speaks with clarity about the extent to which our political and educational leaders are seeking to, in her terms, *"re-order the common language to suit [their] own ideological preferences."* The speed with which this is happening is actually a bit terrifying—more so even than a ride down the Colorado River in early spring.

Secondly, I have included this piece to remind us that these are the people who have been shaping the education and worldviews of our children for several generations now and will continue to do so into the future. Of course, not everyone in education has embraced this revolution. Not everyone in France embraced that revolution. The price for failing to do so, then as now, however, was and is high. In our current context it may not cost you your life, but it can certainly cost you your job.

I am certain that some will see a bit of an overreaction. I would respond by saying that people like Peggy Noonan and John Stonestreet of the Colson Center and Eric Metaxas and Os Guinness and Thomas Sowell and the late Philip Johnson and a host of others are not given to irrational overreaction. In reality we've been on this trajecto-

ry for a long time. In fact, the singular difference between this present time and virtually any time over the last four or five decades is only the pace and radicalism of change.

If we want to get back to an approach to schooling that better represents the purposes of our Lord in this world, we've got to begin by asking and answering the simplest question: Why?

## Why Asking Why Is So Essential

What's the question nearly every one of us first asked? Was it, "What's for dinner?"
How about, "What's the weather going to be today?" Or, "What's the price of that
doggy in the window?" Probably not. Most likely it was the simple, yet powerful question, "Why?"

What's more, it's probably not just the first question we ask but also likely our
most frequently posed question throughout life. If you doubt that assertion, just consider any recent tragedy you have observed or experienced. In nearly every case, what
do people want to know? What do you want to know? Isn't it almost always the question, "Why?" Why would something like this happen? Why would someone want to
do something so awful? Or perhaps your question was the familiar, "Why would a
good God allow such evil?" It is an understandable question, actually. Even the most
faithful among us often wonder at the capacity for evil we see unleashed in the world
around us that injures so many innocent people.

The question of why serves another important purpose, however. Asking why also
helps us better understand the rationale that underlies the things we do in our everyday life. Indeed, I would argue that until we get at the why behind the what in all we
do on an everyday basis, we will find ourselves struggling to effectively fulfill God's
purpose in our lives. That question applies fully to this discussion on the education of
our children.

As we begin this journey to discover what the Scriptures have to say about the why
behind the what of education, I want to clarify something I believe to be important.
While it is true that the Bible says little about schools as institutions, it does have quite
a bit to say about "schooling." Indeed, I acknowledge that nowhere in the Scripture do
we find an exhortation directed at parents encouraging them to enroll their children
in any particular kind of school.

The reason for that should be obvious. At the time the Old Testament Scriptures
were written, schools for the masses were unknown. Most schooling took place in the

home, and for a few fortunate, wealthy families, special tutors were employed. It wasn't until the Greco-Roman age that schooling was a bit more generally available, but even then, usually only to the sons of wealthy and influential families.

Publicly funded, mandated schooling as we know it in our time was actually an idea that took root during the Reformation in Germany. In fact, as noted by historian F. V. N. Painter, "[Martin] Luther deserves henceforth to be recognized as the greatest, not only of religious, but of educational reformers."[5]

As another historian has observed, "There can be no doubt, that Luther the educational reformer, contributed to the modern world not only by insisting that basic education be available to all—and by making it so—but also by bringing to common people the fundamental notion that true religion could be a matter of the mind as well as of the heart and public behavior."[6]

Luther, however, fully understood the interconnected role of church, family, and schooling. "When schools prosper," he observed, "the Church remains righteous and her doctrine pure. . . . Young pupils and students are the seed and source of the Church. If we are dead, whence would come our successors, if not from the schools? For the sake of the Church we must have and maintain Christian schools."[7]

If the great reformer could see this so clearly, why has our vision of the purpose of education been so dimmed? The answer lies in a simple reality. We have ignored and misunderstood the clear meaning of Paul's instruction to the church found in Romans 12:1–2 to not allow the world system to crush us into its mold. Thus, our thinking about schooling has been far more influenced by cultural norms and personal histories than by the teaching of Scripture.

So, while the Scriptures may not speak directly about schools, they do specifically address the why behind the what for all educational endeavors. To begin making my case I want to explore what I believe to be the key text on the why and what of an education designed to equip our children and young people for a life of authentic faith.

## A Unifying Approach to Life

At the heart of the Old Testament Scriptures are five books we commonly refer to as the Wisdom Literature: Job, Psalms, Proverbs, Ecclesiastes, and the Song of Solomon. Each has its own focus. Job, for example, is occupied by a deep philosophical conversation. Ecclesiastes is, in my opinion, one of the most interesting sociological studies of all time. Proverbs, which sits in the middle of the Wisdom Literature, is a book focused on what we would today call common sense. It provides wisdom, insight, and practical instruction on how followers of Jehovah should make their way forward in this broken world.

In his commentary on Proverbs, Derek Kidner describes the book in the following manner. "The samples of behavior which it holds up to view are all assessed by one criterion, which could be summed up in the question, 'Is this wisdom or folly?' This is a unifying approach to life, because it suits the most commonplace realm as fully as the most exalted. Wisdom leaves its signature on anything well-made or well-judged, from an apt remark to the universe itself, from a shrewd policy (which springs from practical insight) to a noble action (which presupposes moral and spiritual discernment). In other words, it is equally at home in the realms of nature and art, of ethics and politics, to mention no others, and forms a single basis of judgment for them all."[8]

I love and embrace that insight. Clearly, Kidner is suggesting that there is a biblical way of thinking and acting about every aspect of life under the sun. Today we would call that idea a biblical worldview. And, as both David and Solomon would tell us, the only "authentic" starting place for that journey is to be found in these words: *the fear of God.*[9]

The implications of that statement are simple to grasp. All wisdom. All knowledge. All understanding. All that matters in how we choose to live life under the sun cannot be fully comprehended until we begin with the realization that God has spoken in an authoritative manner about what is good, and beautiful, and true about all of life.

J. I. Packer speaks to this point when he writes, "Two facts about the triune Jehovah are assumed, if not actually stated in every single biblical passage. The first is that He is king—absolute monarch of the universe ordering all its affairs, working out His will in all that happens within it. The second is that He speaks—uttering words that express His will in order to cause it to be done."[10]

I would encourage you to ponder those words for a moment. God does not speak to hear Himself talk. He speaks to mankind with the express intent that we will hear His words and act on them. How can God's people respond to His word when the opportunity to hear that word is so very limited, as has become the case in our modern, postmodern, highly secularized world?

The grave problem with secular education is not that it leads to an inferior educational experience. Indeed, it is undoubtedly true that when it comes to curriculum and instruction there are many exceptional secular schools. In fact, it is an unfortunate and sad reality that secular schools often outperform Christian schools when it comes to the academic accomplishments of their students.

This should be a challenge to schools that claim to provide a Christ-centered education, and one of the primary reasons Christian parents often choose a secular alternative for their children. I would go so far as to suggest, however, that a school cannot call itself a truly Christlike school unless it pursues its mission fully committed to excellence in all things.

No, the grave problem for secular educational institutions isn't their inability to deliver academic excellence; rather, it is their unwillingness to invite God into the great conversations of our day, whether that conversation is focusing on social justice, the environment, the role of government in the lives of its citizens, our understanding about what is good, true, and beautiful, the nature of human sexuality, or the very nature of life itself.

You could easily add to that list with but a bit of reflection. The salient point here is this: *Secular education excludes God and His Word and establishes itself as sovereign in His place.* In other words, secular authority has chosen to "gag God" by excluding Him from the place where most of our children and young people are being educated. He gets to speak, of course, but only in limited settings and under strict control.

That sobering and uncontested reality should be problematic for anyone who identifies as a follower of Jesus Christ for several reasons. First of all, we should be concerned about what is called in educational theory the null curriculum—a theory that simply notes that students learn as much from what they observe as they do from what they are told. Does that surprise you? Of course not.

Thus, I pose this question to every parent, to every pastor, to every teacher: What conclusion do you think a child is likely to reach about the nature and reality of God after twelve to sixteen years of secular education during which God is never invited to any discussion on any topic of importance? In most cases I would argue that what they typically conclude, consciously or unconsciously, is the following: *God must not have anything of value to add to those conversations.*

I would never discount the impact of parents or the church on the thinking of a student. I would, however, ask parents and pastors to consider this simple fact. Our children and young adults hear so much more from their teachers, from their peers, and from media than they will typically hear from their parents and their pastors.

Consider the implications of this simple math:

- 47. The total number of *hours* the typical evangelical kid spends at his or her church over the course of an entire *year*.
- 7. The number of *hours* the typical evangelical kid spends with media every single *day* of the week, and some research suggests the number of hours could be 10 hours or more per day. Do the math. That means media: *2,555 hours*, church 47 hours. Who wins that contest?
- 15. The number of *minutes* the typical dad of the typical evangelical kid spends in genuine face-to-face conversation with his kid over the course of a *day*.
- 7.5. The *hours* a day the typical evangelical kid spends in school for 180 days every year. Let's do the math. Dad :41 hours a year; school: *1,350 hours*.

So, while I would never devalue the impact of parents and church in the lives of kids, I can do the math. Now I know those numbers vary widely from family to family. I also know, however, it isn't a contest once our kids head off to school. Failure to understand the sheer power of such an imbalance of time is having a catastrophically negative impact on the thinking and behavior of our kids.

Secondly, we should be equally concerned about the power of the culture to "crush people into its mold." So many in the church, however, seem unconvinced (or worse, unconcerned) about the power of culture to shape how we, and our children, see the world. Remember my story of Arnold Palmer, how his life was fundamentally shaped by immersion in his father's world. Do you, as a pastor, as a parent, really believe that daily immersion in our profoundly secular culture won't shape how our children see the world around them?

If you're not sure how you would answer that question, I would ask you to consider these thoughts from James K. A. Smith. "We need to become aware of our immersions. 'This is water,' and you've been swimming in it your whole life. We need to recognize that our imaginations and longings are not impervious to our environments and only informed by our (supposedly 'critical') thinking. To the contrary, our loves and imaginations are conscripted by all sorts of liturgies that are loaded with a vision of the good life. To be immersed in those 'secular' liturgies is to be habituated to long for what they promise."[11] What a powerful observation—one to which we should pay careful attention.

Culture is a powerful influence on all of our lives, and far more so today than at any other time in the history of our country, if for no other reason than the pervasive nature of media. Anyone who would suggest that our kids are not vulnerable to the constant, clever, intrusive messaging bombarding them from every possible source is either remarkably naïve or willfully ignorant of current reality.

Thirdly, we must stop ignoring the fact that education is never, and I mean never, simply an exercise in objective reporting. It is rare to find anyone who is at all objective in his or her presentations. Educators and the education they provide are never value-neutral. All of us are biased in one way or another, and hiding those biases is a near impossibility. We might be able to control what we say in certain situations. In a secular education setting, however, the curriculum will typically introduce arguments consistent with a secular, naturalistic worldview that neither teachers nor students are any longer free to question.

I've often noted that few people have a greater impact on a child than a "winsome pagan." By using that phrase, I am not suggesting that teachers are pagans in the sense of those marauding Vikings and their pantheon of gods from a millennium ago. It is the case, however, that given a curriculum devoid of any mention of the Creator God, teachers, whether they desire to be or not, become agents of a thoroughly secular worldview. And let's be honest. Nearly every parent has heard his or her child say, "*But my teacher says.*" Teachers have an impact on the thinking of our children, and the impact of great teachers can be huge. No parent should ever underestimate the influence of teachers on the thinking of their children.

Combine the amount of time children spend in schooling with the fact that worldviews and values are *caught* more than *taught*, and we must face the fact that *our children are already being discipled.* And it matters who is doing the discipling, and *what* is being transmitted from adult to child.

## A Parent's Plea

Many, if not most, cultures have, throughout history, practiced what we would call a "rite of passage." Those events were designed to signal that a young person was stepping from childhood into emerging adulthood, from a life of dependency to a life of responsibility. In some cases, the rite of passage could involve some dangerous, even life-threatening elements.

In our modern world that step into greater obligation has become more symbolic in nature. Today's confirmation, bar mitzvah, and graduation ceremonies would be examples of that. While those kinds of observances are important markers along the road to adulthood, they do not always convey the serious nature of the transition taking place. There is seldom any real testing involved or substantial questions asked. Score a grade point average even slightly above failing and you get to walk across the platform, ready or not for what is to follow.

Most ancient societies took this passage a bit more seriously. The book of Proverbs provides us with some insight into how seriously. As we will see a bit later, however, there was no coercion, no "you've got to do this," no get it right or you don't win your badge of honor. There was, however, a serious attempt to provide some substantial guidance about the reality of the life to come with all of its challenges and opportunities and how best to live that life. You could certainly ignore acting on what you were being taught, but you could never say, "I wasn't given fair warning about what lay ahead."

Indeed, in the book of Proverbs, Solomon quickly makes his point in the introduction to this collection of wise sayings and then reinforces it over the next series of chapters. Consider this repeated refrain:

- Hear, my son, your father's instruction, and forsake not your mother's teaching, for they are a graceful garland for your head and pendants for your neck. (Proverbs 1:8–9)
- My son, if you receive my words and treasure up my commandments with you, making your ear attentive to wisdom and inclining your heart to understanding. (Proverbs 2:1–2)
- My son, do not forget my teaching but let your heart keep my commandments. (Proverbs 3:1)
- Hear, O sons, a father's instruction, be attentive, that you may gain insight, for I give you good precepts; do not forsake my teaching. (Proverbs 4:1–2)
- My son, be attentive to wisdom; incline your ear to my understanding, that you may keep discretion, and your lips may guard knowledge. (Proverbs 5:1–2)
- My son, keep my words and treasure up my commandments with you; keep my commandments and live. (Proverbs 7:1–2)
- To you O men, I call, and my cry is to the children of man. O simple ones, learn prudence, O fools, learn sense. Hear, for I will speak noble things, and from my lips will come what is right, for my mouth will utter truth; wickedness is an abomination to my lips. (Proverbs 4–7)

Are you beginning to see a pattern? There is no command here. Rather, this is a plea from parents to sons and daughters, a plea to pursue wisdom and travel the road leading to life. Jesus does much the same thing during His ministry. He never demands. Rather, He invites. "Come unto me all of you who labor and I will give you rest" was His encouragement.

Jesus never covers up the consequences of ignoring His call, but He never forces anyone to embrace that call. Even the ancient Greek philosophers understood this crucial distinction. Plato put it this way: *"Knowledge which is acquired under compulsion obtains no hold on the mind."*[12] This must become the mindset of every Christian school if we are to have the impact on lives that we so desire.

Let's now return to Solomon's opening words, which I believe provide us with a thesis statement for all that is to follow in Proverbs. In this passage, Proverbs 1:1–7, Solomon employs a series of infinitive phrases that present us with a template for Christian schooling. He tells us that we are to:

- know wisdom and instruction. This is the content piece.
- understand words of insight. This is the "What does this mean?" piece.
- receive instruction in wise dealing, in righteousness, justice, and equity. This is the "What must I do with all of this information?" piece.
- give prudence to the simple, knowledge and discretion to the youth. This is the *telos*, the desired-outcome piece.

He then focuses our attention on the foundational truth that "the fear of God is the beginning" of this process. Until we are willing to bow our heart and incline our mind to what God has to say, we will never become all that God intends for us to become. This truth is, as my friend and mentor Bruce Lockerbie has written, the authentic starting place if we want to truly learn to think and act like a Christian.[13]

## The Characters in the Drama

One of the many things that make this text so fascinating to me is the cast of characters to whom we are quickly introduced. Those characters are:

- The simple (1:4)
- The fool (1:7)

- The wise (1:5)
- The scoffer (1:22)

To me the central player in this narrative is the person Solomon identifies as the simple (or the naïve, depending on the translation). It is primarily to this individual that Solomon directs his teaching. In both cases, however, the word used in the text comes from an ancient Hebrew word meaning an open door. Over time it came to refer to what we today would call an open mind. To the ancient Hebrews the idea of an open mind was not viewed positively. Indeed, to them an open mind, like an open door, was an invitation for disaster.

The ancient Hebrews, however, were not advocates of a closed mind either. For example, Solomon observes that, "The simple [those with an open mind] tend to believe everything, but the prudent gives thought to his steps."[14] Now imagine the havoc that is created in the mind of young people who head off to college being told that an open mind is the goal for which they must strive. In reality we don't have to imagine that scenario. It plays out in front of us day after day in colleges and universities all across our country.

Every parent, every pastor, should be concerned about the context in which children and young adults learn because, as Solomon notes, "Whoever walks with the wise becomes wise, but the companion of fools will suffer harm."[15] Or consider this insight: "A fool takes no pleasure in understanding, but only in expressing his opinion. When wickedness comes, contempt comes also, and with dishonor comes disgrace."[16] I must confess that I am puzzled by why parents would want to expose their children to a daily barrage of foolishness in the form of secular education.

The Hebrews rejected both the open mind and the closed mind, instead seeking to develop a discerning mind. In Christian schooling, in whatever form it takes, that should be the goal as well. To accomplish that outcome requires a lively give-and-take between teacher and student that asks of both a bit of humility coupled with a willingness to hear the arguments of others.

Again, I'll ask you to consider the following from the pen of Solomon. "Before destruction a man's heart is haughty, but humility comes before honor. If one gives an answer before he hears, it is his folly and shame. An intelligent heart acquires knowledge, and the ear of the wise seeks knowledge."[17] Failure to understand and practice what Solomon shares here is a grave threat to quality education, whether in a secular or sacred setting. To be wise in one's own eyes is to be a fool in the eyes of God and to do great harm to others.

While the specific age of the "simple" isn't mentioned, it is fascinating that most rites of passage, in most cultures, in most eras, occurred during the early teen years. Thus, one thing we might want to ponder is why we, in our current age, so often allow such a long, and frankly unhealthy, extension of childhood and adolescence.

Wouldn't it make sense to elevate, rather than lower, our expectations for more mature understanding and behavior from our young people? I believe that is the argument that Solomon is making throughout Proverbs. Perhaps we should follow his lead in this regard. Perhaps we ought to speak to our young people with the same kind of honesty that characterizes what Solomon has to say in the Proverbs.

Perhaps we should. Will we?

A key to understanding Proverbs is the simple truth that the more we parents can expose our young people to wise thinking and wise people, the greater positive impact we can have on their beliefs and behavior. Conversely the greater exposure our young people have to the foolish and scoffers, the more opportunity for harm exists.[18]

## So, Ultimately, What Is the Why Behind the What?

I hope by now the answer to that question has become obvious. If not, however, permit me another quick story. In the mid-1970s while teaching high school Bible at a Christian school in south Florida, I decided to take what was, at the time, a radical step. While teaching through the book of Proverbs, I decided to add a sex education component to my curriculum. As I said, it was something quite unusual in a Christian school at that moment in history, but it seemed to make a lot of sense to me, so I plunged in.

At the heart of my curriculum was a three-part series of cassette tapes (remember those?) titled The Virginity Question, delivered by R. C. Sproul. In those presentations Sproul began by outlining the typical evangelical arguments for remaining pure until marriage. He then did something quintessentially Sproulian: He demolished the arguments he had just made. It was quite brilliant, actually, but it created a bit of dissonance for my students.

They already knew the arguments. They had heard them repeatedly from their parents and pastors. Now here they were having those very arguments demolished by a leading theologian. You could see the looks on their faces—"What's up with this?" As you can imagine, we had some interesting conversations.

In his final presentation, Dr. Sproul recapped all he had taught to that point and then brought the entire argument to its conclusion with a statement that went something like this: Sexual relations outside of marriage are wrong simply because God says, "NO!" It is that clear. It is that simple. It isn't open to debate. God has spoken on the matter. We can obey His command regarding sexual activity, or we can ignore and thus disobey His command. There are no other options for those who call themselves disciples of Christ.

In a society so saturated by sexual imagery and calls for sexual "liberation" as ours is, acting in obedience to the clear teaching of Scripture regarding sexual conduct can be hard. Anyone with a heartbeat realizes that. Because sexual purity is so difficult to practice in our culture, however, does not lessen our obligation to obey the clear commands of Scripture.

So back to my question: What's the why behind the what of schooling? What authority should shape our actions as parents and pastors? Should it be the norms of culture, or should it be the mandates of Scripture? I hope that the answer has become obvious. When God instructs Israel through Moses to immerse children in the Word of God, He is not asking them to sprinkle a bit of truth into the periphery of their life; rather, He is demanding that they be saturated with truth on a daily basis.

When the apostle Paul instructs parents to "bring up their children in the *paideia* of Christ," that is not a suggestion. It is a mandate. We may employ different means to fulfill that obligation, but we may not simply ignore that responsibility, nor may we outsource that task to people who will systematically expose our children and young people to the most grievous error. That is not an option given us by our Lord.

I know that everyone reading this book wants to see our children and young people become more like Christ in every aspect of their lives. We want them to become discerning, devoted disciples whose decisions and actions are shaped by their love for Christ, for His Word, and for His work in the world.

That is a tall order. It is something that has always been difficult to achieve. Given the intensifying influences of a culture unmoored from true truth, coupled with the current reality that both parents and pastors are less able to engage, for a whole lot of reasons, in the day-to-day lives of their children, it has become an even greater challenge. Perhaps it's time to acknowledge a simple fact: We can't do it alone. We need help if we are to ensure that our children and our young people receive an education that falls fully under the Lordship of Jesus Christ. Doing otherwise is just not an option.

In the following chapters, I will attempt to outline a way forward, a way to construct a "what" that will allow us to accomplish our "why."

## For Reflection

1. What are the fundamental presuppositions that shape your understanding of how you believe your child should be educated? How do those presuppositions align with the ideas presented in this chapter?

2. Agree or disagree: Current cultural norms as promoted in America's publicly funded schools and through much of media are in clear conflict with biblical norms. Does that concern you? Why or why not? How should you respond to that reality?

3. What is your answer to this question? What is the fundamental purpose of education? How would your answer to that question impact how you as a parent and a pastor chose to educate your child?

4. Were you aware that Martin Luther, the great reformer, is considered the "greatest, not only of religious, but educational reform"? How does schooling relate to family and church in the task of disciple making today?

5. Respond to, and consider the ramifications of, this observation by Luther: "When schools prosper the church remains righteous and her doctrine pure . . . Young pupils and students are the seed and source of the Church. If we are dead, whence would come our successors, if not from the schools?"

6. If the fear of God is the beginning of wisdom, knowledge, and understanding, is it possible to provide a genuine education that ignores the reality and authority of God? How should that fact impact your thinking on the education of our children?

Chapter 5

## Weaving the Fabric of Faithfulness

If you are in any way a person who loves the out-of-doors, you are probably familiar with a wonderful fabric called Gore-Tex. The Gore-Tex Company was founded in 1957 by Bill Gore, who had served as a chemist with the DuPont Corporation. He was convinced that he could find more applications for one of DuPont's most well-known products, Teflon. He experienced some success, but the company really took off when his son Bob discovered a way to heat and stretch Teflon just the right amount to create a waterproof-yet-breathable fabric that was to revolutionize outdoor gear.

Gore-Tex has been used in the production of tents, shoes, socks, hats, coats, gloves, and a host of other outdoor merchandise. I have much personal experience with Gore-Tex products and can say with absolute confidence that they work as advertised. It is a truly incredible invention. I once stood in a deer stand for an entire late November morning in constant cold drizzle wearing Gore-Tex boots, coat, and hat and never once felt discomfort because of the rain or temperature. And never once had to wipe the rain off my glasses.

Whether it is rain gear, comfortable cotton sheets, a favorite wool sweater, or a brightly colored silk blouse, all of us have experienced the remarkable results of someone who at some time learned the best way to weave a fabric into something of extraordinary value and usefulness. As Bob Gore discovered, however, it can take some thought and experimentation to discover how best to employ the materials and systems available in a manner that produces the desired outcome.

If, as I have argued, the outcome we should desire for our children is a life that accurately and courageously reflects the image of Christ, then it would make sense to discover the best way to fashion the fabric for that life from what God has revealed of Himself in His Word and in His world. It is something about which I have given much thought throughout my adult life. For me it has been a personal and professional quest. Personal in the sense that I realized from my study of Scripture that I couldn't pass on to my students something I did not embrace myself—no one can. As the apostle Paul observed, how could I provide to others what I myself did not possess?[1] And professional because I had chosen to become a teacher and I didn't want to waste my effort in pursuit of a philosophy or practice that wasn't likely to achieve my desired outcome: the transformation of my students into people who would accurately reflect the person of Christ.

As much as it pains me to say this, I must confess that like Bob Gore, I found myself failing more often than not. I got some things right, but I sensed that there was some secret sauce missing from my efforts. I loved my students and the men in our church I was led to disciple. I really did. I understood that without the Word and the Spirit, my efforts would be less than effective. I realized that as a teacher and a pastor I had to prepare well to teach well. I came to realize, however, that discipling required more, way more, than serving as the proverbial "sage on the stage." It took me some time, however, to begin to see how it all fit together.

When I wrote my books on school finance and strategic planning, I was quick to note that I was nowhere close to the leading expert on either topic. I confess the same here. There are many who have addressed the idea of how to be effective as a teacher and discipler with far greater insight than I.[2] I have, however, developed some thoughts on how best to weave the fabric of faithfulness together into the life of a student that I want to share in this and the following two chapters.

As I begin, I want to express my thanks to some of those who have most influenced me along the way on this journey, and in the process to recommend some exceptional books written by those individuals. I have had the opportunity to develop a personal relationship with some of those people. Others have influenced me through their research, writing, and speaking. I long ago learned to embrace something I read in a book by one of those people, Howard Hendricks. In his book *Teaching to Change Lives* he observed, "If you stop growing today, you stop teaching tomorrow."[3] I fully believe in that observation and have used it to shape how and with whom I spend my time each week.

The first person on that list is Bruce Lockerbie. I first encountered Dr. Lockerbie at a conference in Lancaster, Pennsylvania, when I was a struggling head of school. Few people have so immediately impressed me in the manner he did as I sat through his workshops. I had previously read a book he had written, *Thinking and Acting Like a Christian*. It was in that book that I discovered the idea, so important to our work as teachers, that we must find the authentic starting place for our efforts, the idea I addressed in chapter four. As Dr. Lockerbie reminded me, that starting place was revealed in these words: "The fear of God is the beginning of wisdom."[4]

Others who influenced me were Francis Schaeffer in his many books, especially *The God Who Is There*; Os Guiness; Frank Gaebelein in *The Pattern of God's Truth*; John Richard Neuhaus; Rockne McCarthy, Donald Oppewal, Walfred Peterson, and Gordon Spykman, authors of *Society, State, and School and Disestablishment a Second Time*; the exceptional constitutional attorney William Bently Ball, who wrote *Mere Creatures of the State*; Donavan Graham, author of *Teaching Redemptively*; James K. A. Smith, author of *Desiring the Kingdom*; Nancy Pearcy, author of *Total Truth*; and J. P. Moreland, especially his book *Loving God with All Your Mind*.

The person, however, who helped crystalize all that I had read and studied into a helpful framework was Dr. Steven Garber in his truly important book *The Fabric of Faithfulness: Weaving Together Belief and Behavior During the University Years*. As I read his book, I realized that there was no single way forward in this thing we call Christian schooling. Rather we, as teachers, are required to think about how a number of different threads must be woven together for us to achieve our ultimate goal. His thoughts, along with the others I have already mentioned, have helped focus my thinking and will shape the contours of this book, especially over this and the next two chapters.

## The Tragic Disconnect

You can and should read Dr. Garber's book to discover what prompted the study that forms the basis for what he has to say. I think, however, that the following lengthy quote will reveal the key question that impelled his research.

> Many students, perhaps most, emerge from their university experience ready to take on the world; the idealism of youth we call it. But then somewhere along the way the reality of life in the fast lane of adult responsibility hits—sometimes like a ton of bricks, sometimes like acid rain. In a thousand ways they see how hard it is to be faithful to family, at work, in politics. Day in and day out they experience disappointments in every part of life—every part of life—and see how hard it is to be hopeful (and therefore responsible) actors in human history as they

try to be neighbors to those next door and to those around the world.

The cartoon "Non Sequitur" captures this brilliantly, allowing us to smile even as we see its sober realities. Titled "Post Graduation," it shows the hallway of an academic building with an open classroom door identified by the words REAL LIFE 101. Six feet below, an undergraduate is lying face down on the sidewalk, smashed flat against the concrete, his papers strewn all about. Nearby is a sign that reads: WARNING. NO LIFEGUARD ON DUTY EVER.

And yet there are students who come through that crucible with habits of the heart and mind so in place that they move on into the responsibilities and privileges of adulthood without compromising their basic integrity or giving in to the cynicism of 'realpolitik,' 'realeconomik,' or 'realaesthetik' (and I might add without the kind of gender and identity confusion so prevalent on our campuses today).

Who are they? What happens during their university years that so forms their vision and virtues that they make it through the proverbial "valley of diapers" of their twenties and thirties with their convictions and character intact? *How does a person decide which cares and commitments will give shape to life, for life? How do students learn to conscientiously connect what they believe about the world with how they live in the world?*[5] [My emphasis.]

That is the question all of us—parents, pastors, and educators—must answer. It isn't enough to simply send them off to "school" and hope that somehow, in God's sovereign will, everything will turn out all right. Such thinking isn't biblical. In fact, it's as far from biblical as you can get. I've searched the Scriptures pretty diligently to find the text that says, "Go ahead and ignore what I'm teaching you. It doesn't really matter because it will all work out in the end anyway." It does matter what we do and how we do what we do. In fact, in this case, it matters a lot.

Dr. Garber's book, by the way, was published in 1996. In 2020, things have gotten exponentially more challenging for our children and hugely more important for how we choose to educate them. Indeed, as many books and articles make clear, the threat to our children is greater today than it has been in generations, and yet sadly our response by any rational accounting has been more tepid and less effective than at any time over that same period. That is another reason behind this book. If we don't change our strategy, we are likely to end up like those brave cavalrymen forever memorialized in Alfred Lord Tennyson's poem *The Charge of the Light Brigade*.

By the way, if you can remember the opening lines of that poem you probably need to thank a teacher.

## Seven Necessary Threads

It is my goal, therefore, in this and the following two chapters, to argue that without a truly Christian approach to education, it is supremely difficult to fulfill our responsibility to raise up a generation of young people who biblically understand how to "conscientiously connect what they believe about the world with how they live in the world," as Dr. Garber puts it.

To accomplish that goal, I have identified seven threads that must be well-woven together if we hope to create a durable fabric of faithfulness of sufficient strength to withstand the stresses of life in a fallen world. Those threads are:

- A Real-World Faith
- A Reasonable Faith
- An Integrated Faith
- An Embodied Faith
- A Willing Faith
- A Communal Faith
- A Consuming Faith

## First Thread: A Real-World Faith

I've placed this at the very beginning to allow me to address one of the most persistent and flawed arguments against Christian schooling and schools. It goes something like this. Our kids need to experience the real world. Hiding them away in a "bubble" does a disservice to them and will handicap them in life.

I recently heard that argument at a conference for Christian school leaders, advanced by a Christian who works in the public schools. She tried her best to soften her statements in front of this particular audience, but it was clear she believed that children and young people enrolled in Christian schools or homeschooled miss out on essential life lessons. Interestingly, some in the room were nodding their heads in agreement.

In response, let me say first of all that anyone who believes that the American public school at any level is representative of "real life" is self-deceived. Contemporary American public schools are about as far from real life as one can get. Yes, schools are in many ways a reflection of life in America today. That doesn't make them real, however, and may help explain why so many graduates find it difficult to move on into adulthood and its attendant responsibilities.[6]

In reality, Christian schooling is not a bubble. Rather it is, or should be, a boot camp. Reflecting on my earlier chapters, Christian schooling is about equipping children and young people to engage in the war that is raging all around them. Doing that takes time and specific preparation. To simply send anyone into battle without adequate preparation and effective tools is a crime.

Even the Marine Corps diligently and thoroughly prepares its recruits before subjecting them to live-fire drills. The idea that you can just drop someone into combat without that preparation is folly. Indeed, I don't know of any reputable mission agency that would send someone to India or Brazil or Tanzania or Pakistan without extensive preparation and without careful vetting to ensure that a candidate is actually ready for the challenges ahead. And even when they do all of that, the recidivism rate is high for first-time missionaries.

Somehow, however, evangelical pastors and parents have come to accept that it's not only OK but a good idea to drop our kids into the combat zone that America's public schools have become. I get that the American public school is in desperate need of the gospel. Two facts must, however, be considered. First, for reasons that are beyond my comprehension, our legal system has decided to do everything possible to eliminate any vestige of faith from the curriculum and practice of public schools. Second, if missionaries are to be sent into this environment, then we should send those who are best prepared for the work.

I would argue that those would be adults such as teachers and administrators. Are there some young people who are ready for the task? Possibly, though I suspect that if the research is accurate those kinds of young people are few in number. Could churches do a better job of providing the right kind of preparation and support for those students? Certainly. And perhaps it is being done. I'm just not familiar with those efforts.

Even so, I am constrained by David's observations in Psalm 1 that the blessed man is the one

> who walks not in the counsel of the wicked
> nor stands in the way of sinners,
> nor sits in the seat of scoffers
> but his delight is in the law of the Lord
> and on his law he mediates day and night.

I struggle to reconcile those words with the idea of prematurely placing vulnerable children and young people into a context in which they will be daily confronted with unwise counsel from those who scoff at the very idea of true truth and the One who is the author of that true truth. Doing so makes no sense to me and seems to clearly contradict the teaching of Scripture.

Those of us engaged in Christian schooling in all forms recognize that one of our primary responsibilities, and thus one of our key goals, is the preparation of children and young people for the battle in which they will engage on a daily basis. We recognize that that battle takes place in the "real world" of commerce, culture, and community. We are just reluctant to send off ill-equipped little missionaries only to watch them become casualties of the battle for which we failed to prepare them.[7]

If we are to prepare our students for life in the "real world," we must first understand what is actually happening in that world. It is hard to prepare someone for a task without a clear understanding of what that task entails and the context in which they will be engaging in that task. Repairing a car engine in a clean, climate-controlled facility is, for example, a bit different from attempting to repair a life-preserving oxygen scrubber in a broken space capsule while hurtling through space, as was required during the Apollo 13 flight to the moon. You just can't ignore context.

## The Worst Hard Time

In his fascinating book *The Worst Hard Time*, Timothy Egan provides some insight into that reality. He tells the story of the Dust Bowl, one of the worst ecological disasters in modern American history. In that book he gives a vivid description of what became known as Black Sunday.

Bam White saw this black monstrosity approaching from the south, and he thought at first he was looking at a range of mountains on the move, nearly two miles high. But the Llano Estacado was one of the flattest places on earth, and there was no mountain ten thousand feet high, moving or stationary, anywhere on the horizon. . . . "What is it?" Mel White asked his daddy. "It's the earth, itself," Bam said. "The earth is on the move."[8]

That was Black Sunday, April 14, 1935, the day of the worst duster of them all: The storm carried twice as much dirt as was dug out to create the Panama Canal. The canal took seven years to dig; the storm lasted a single afternoon. More than 300,000 tons of Great Plains topsoil was airborne that day.[9] Try to wrap your mind around that scene.

There has been lots of speculation as to what led to the events of that day. Some have suggested it was the result of a lengthy drought. Others have speculated poor crop management.[10] Had such an event happened today, climate change would most likely top the list of probable causes. In reality the reason was something much more prosaic. See below for the weapon of mass destruction that helped create the catastrophe described by Egan.

Surprised? Yes, believe it or not, the primary culprit creating the disaster we remember as the Dust Bowl was a run-of-the-mill tractor. Permit me to explain what Egan discovered in the research for his book.

As the railroads pushed westward, one of the ways the owners of those railroad lines discovered to generate sustainable income was in developing a way to help farmers get their crops to the market. In the late 19th century, there was plenty of cheap land available on the Great Plains, and plenty of people who wanted to make a living farming that land. With the coming of the railroad, the problem of how to get crops to the market was solved. In the process, however, a greater problem was created: the destruction of the Great Plains ecosystem.

It wasn't a deliberate destruction. It happened, inadvertently, because those farmers had no idea of what they were doing when they plowed up land about which they knew little or nothing. The Great Plains was unlike anything the typical farmer from the East Coast or Midwest had ever encountered. Like the Lewis and Clark expedition, they were in a world for which they had no real precedent, and their past experiences did not adequately prepare them for what they were now experiencing.

If that sounds familiar, it should. Much of what we face today while seeking to prepare and equip our children and young adults for life in this flawed and fallen world requires us to think differently than we have till now. And it's only going to become more challenging.

As Timothy Egan points out regarding the Great Plains, "Through all of the seasonal tempests, man was inconsequential. As long as the weave of grass was stitched to the land the prairie would flourish in dry years and wet. The grass could look brown and dead, but beneath the surface, the roots held the soil in place; it was alive."[11]

All of that changed, however, with the arrival of thousands of farmers who soon had access to a new invention: the gasoline-powered tractor. Tractors could plow up multiple more acres in any given day than horse-drawn plows. As long as sufficient rain fell, things went well. When the inevitable drought came, however, the result was devastating.

This is an important lesson for us. Drought is inevitable. Disaster is not. Dry days will come. They may persist for months, even years. But you can survive as long as your root system remains healthy and unbroken. Fail to cultivate the "web of life," however, and you will find yourself driven before the wind, living a life of frustration, futility, and fury.

Consider the simple comparison between the image of a tree planted by streams of water that remains fruitful and the dry and the lifeless chaff that the wind effortlessly drives away, which David employs in Psalm 1. What is the difference? In the case of the tree, the roots go deep and thus the tree is sustained even in times of drought. Chaff, like leaves that detach from a tree as winter approaches, has no connection to anything capable of sustaining life. Chaff is rootless, driven by every unpredictable gust of wind, unable to do more than respond to forces beyond its control. It is a desperate kind of existence.

That, sadly, is what happens to so many of our young people. Severed from the true source of life, they are unable to do anything but react to the forces swirling about them. As Steven Garber observes, "Our current social condition—the maelstrom of modernity—makes it incredibly difficult for Christian students to form a life that integrally connects their personal and public worlds."[12]

Now here is the sad fact that makes that reality almost inevitable. "Characteristically, it isn't that they choose to disconnect; rather it is in the very air they breathe as they grow up in America."[13]

In a more recent study, Dr. Christian Smith makes a similar observation. "The cultural ocean in which American adolescents swim saturates them in the ethos of therapeutic individualism."[14] He then goes on to explain. "Therapeutic individualism defines the individual self as the source and standard of authentic moral knowledge and authority, and individual self-fulfillment as the preoccupying purpose of life. Subjective, personal experience is the touchstone of all that is authentic, right, and true. By contrast, this ethos views the 'external' traditions, obligations, and institutions of society as inauthentic and often illegitimate constraints on morality and behavior from which individuals must be emancipated."[15]

Even more troubling is how Smith describes the low level of biblical knowledge possessed by the typical American teenager, including those who attend our conservative evangelical churches. He writes, "Again, nobody expects adolescents to be sophisticated theologians. But very few of the descriptions of personal beliefs offered by the teenagers we interviewed, especially the Christian teenagers, come close to representing marginally coherent accounts of the basic, important religious beliefs of their own faith traditions. The majority of U.S. teens would badly fail a hypothetical short-answer or essay test of the basic beliefs of their religion."[16]

I'll return to Dr. Smith's research in the next chapter. For now, it is important to note the difference in the two studies. Steven Garber was looking at students who had graduated from college in the 1970s and 1980s. Christian Smith was focusing on students who were still in high school in the first decade of the 21st century. My point? The challenges plaguing college students thirty and forty years ago are now afflicting kids who are much younger and much less-prepared for what they face on a day-to-day basis. If we aren't concerned about where all of this is leading, we should be.

Put another way, we live in an era of chaotic discontinuity. It is a moment in time during which the very fundamentals and foundations of life are under relentless assault in every context, especially in two inescapable settings: school and media, with one constantly reinforcing the other day in and day out. What was commonly accepted by the vast majority of Americans of all stripes and beliefs only a few decades ago is now called anathema by those who shape what and how we teach our students.

It is a time when, as a culture, we have decided to call evil good and good evil.[17] Think of how difficult that is for you. Now imagine how problematic it is for kids who are not yet prepared to think with discernment about all they hear every day from their teachers, their peers, and the relentless pounding of media.

Before addressing the other six threads I see as crucial to the process of weaving the fabric of faithfulness in the lives of our children and young people, permit me one final observation.

## Sink or Swim

My dad, being a former Marine—no that's wrong, there are no former Marines; as the saying goes, "Once a Marine always a Marine"—had a particular way of teaching his sons about life. As someone who had faced death over and over again and had had to control his fear in the face of those circumstances, my dad saw it as his responsibility to teach my brother and me that same control. His methodology was, however, not always the best, and as a result, though I eventually "got" the goal, I'm probably lucky to still be alive to tell this story.

I can't remember exactly when the event I'm going to describe took place, but it was before junior high (that's what we once called grades seven–nine). I do remember where we were: standing on the edge of a bluff overlooking the Medina River in the Hill Country of central Texas. We were probably only ten feet above the surface of the river, but to my eyes it looked a whole lot steeper. At that moment my dad encouraged me to do a backflip into the water below. It isn't that I hadn't ever dived into the water before. I had done so many times into a pool. A backflip from a bluff into a river, however, was beyond my experience. I wasn't really interested in pursuing my dad's suggestion. But you know how it is: you've got to prove You've got what it takes. So, I stepped to the edge of the bluff, turned my back to the river below, and launched myself into space.

Obviously, I survived the experience. Barely. The pain from landing body and face first, however, still resonates every time I recall that incident. From ten feet up, water is not soft. It isn't exactly like hitting cement, but you would never have convinced me of that fact at that time. Here was the problem. I had never been given any real instructions about how to perform a backflip, how to control the flip. As a consequence, I managed to over-flip before hitting the surface of the water. What I can tell you is that it was a very long time before I ever tried that stunt again.

If you are or have ever been a parent, your response to my father's actions might be pretty harsh. You might be thinking that no parent should ever put a child at that kind of risk. And I would agree with you. We should never ask our children to do something for which they are not fully and adequately prepared. They might survive the situation, but that isn't the point. You don't put your children at risk for no compelling reason.

And yet that is exactly what we do when we send our children into a battle for their minds and hearts they are not prepared to wage. It's why Jesus speaks so harshly to those who would "cause a little one to stumble" and why the apostle Paul warns of how vulnerable children are to "human cunning and deceitful schemes."[18] You may not agree with me that Christ-centered schooling, as I am describing it in this book, is mandated by the Scriptures. Hopefully, however, you will fully embrace your responsibility to find a way to adequately prepare the children over whom you have been given a stewardship responsibility for the battle into which they have been thrust.

It's a tough world out there. Thus, we have an obligation to muster all available resources to equip them with the kind of real-world faith they will need to survive and thrive in that world. Remember: You can't do it alone.

Now it's on to the remaining threads we want to weave together into the life of faithfulness with which we all hope to clothe our children. And by the way, they are the very same threads pastors need to weave into the lives of those they have been called to shepherd and disciple.

## For Reflection

1. Reread Steven Garber's observation and respond to his question: How does a person decide which cares and commitments will give shape to life, for life? How do students learn to conscientiously connect what they believe about the world with how they live in the world?

2. A Christian school should not be a bubble hiding kids from the world. Rather it should be a boot camp preparing kids to engage the world in its brokenness. Respond.

3. We require so much in the preparation of missionaries. Can we in good conscience do less in the preparation of our children? Is sink or swim really a good strategy? What approach would make more sense?

Chapter 6

## More Threads, More Weaving

Here is a question I often pose to educators: "What do middle school students value more than anything else?" After a bit of discussion, the answer to my question is invariably something like this: "Middle school students value their relationships with friends more than anything else." I think that is correct. It is one of the reasons I believe that peer pressure holds such power over the average middle school and high school kid.

I then always ask a follow-up question. "Why do you believe that those relationships hold such power in the life of a middle school student?" After some additional discussion the group again will almost always settle on the belief that kids somehow find their significance, their identity, through those relationships. At a time when they are beginning to seek their personal identity apart from their parents and family, the place they most typically and naturally turn to find that identity is through their peer relationships.

At that point in the conversation I introduce a concept that I borrowed from a presentation I attended years ago. In that address, Jeff Myers, the current president of Summit Ministries, shared the diagram below.

The point Jeff was making through this diagram was remarkably simple but profoundly insightful. People's behavior is shaped by what they value, whether they

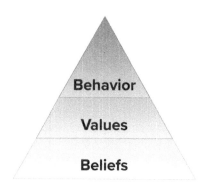

can articulate that value or not, and their values always emerge from what they believe to be true—again whether they can articulate those beliefs or not. Thus, if we attempt to change behavior by focusing only on the behavior itself, we are certainly doomed to failure. People must first see, then understand, what they believe, how those beliefs shape values, and then see and understand how those beliefs and values drive behavior.

Now it is true that our "sin nature" is the ultimate cause for our bad behavior. The flaws in our thinking are, however, the fuel that our sin nature ignites leading to our destructive actions. And like any fire, the more fuel, the greater and more destructive the conflagration.

Thus, if we want to diminish the power of peer pressure, one thing that we must do is to help kids discover a foundational truth: Our identity is in Christ, not in the crowd. Human behavior is often complex and motives are usually muddy, but one thing is true: We are driven by what we value, and those values emerge from what we believe to be true.

For example, the desire for security in one's life is an understandable value. Place too much value in security, however, and, as history demonstrates, people are often willing to put their lives and treasure into the hands of tyrants. This is sadly true for even followers of Jesus Christ who ignore two key truths: First, that God is sovereign in this world, and He works all things out according to His will; and second, that yes, God is sovereign, but that doesn't mean we will always escape the consequences of living in a fallen, unjust world. As the author of Ecclesiastes observed, sometimes the wicked prosper and the righteous suffer.[1] The follower of Christ is not promised a life unaffected by suffering, only that God will be with us as we journey through the valley of the shadow of death.

My point is this—a key thread essential to weaving the fabric of faithfulness is what I will call a reasonable faith.

## Second Thread: A Reasonable Faith

Steven Garber notes that "belief and behavior are braided together in the deepest places in the heart."[2] The beliefs to which he refers are not, however, some generic bumper-sticker clichés. Rather, they are the kind of sound, thoughtful, based-on-unimpeachable-evidence reply that the apostle Paul continually references in his writing and speaking. We see an example of that during his trial before Agrippa and Festus. After a bit of give-and-take, Festus declares, "Paul you are out of your mind; your great learning is driving you out of your mind."[3]

In response to Festus's statement, Paul declares, "I am not out of my mind most excellent Festus but I am speaking true and rational words. For the king knows about these things, and to him I speak boldly. For I am persuaded that none of these things has escaped his notice, for this has not been done in a corner."[4] In short, Paul responds to the skepticism of those in power with a simple statement of known, historical fact.

It is a pattern we observe repeatedly throughout the New Testament epistles. For example, in his first letter to the church in Corinth, in one of the most powerful passages in all of Scripture, Paul places the death and resurrection of Christ in a known historical context. He then goes on to argue, "And if Christ has not been raised, then our preaching is in vain and your faith is in vain. We are even found to be misrepresenting God, because we testified about God that he raised Christ, whom he did not raise if it is true that the dead are not raised. For if the dead are not raised, not even Christ has been raised. And if Christ has not been raised your faith is futile and you are still in your sins. Then those also who have fallen asleep in Christ have perished. If in Christ we have hope in this life only, we are of all people most miserable"[5]

Both the apostles John and Peter use the same line of argument in speaking of Christ. John reminds his readers of a singular reality: "That which was from the beginning, which we heard, which we have seen with our eyes, which we looked upon and have touched with our hands, concerning the word of life—the life was made manifest to us—that we have seen and heard we proclaim also to you, so that you too may have fellowship with us."[6]

Peter takes the same approach in his letters to the churches. He prompts his readers to faith with these words: "For we did not follow cleverly devised myths when we made known to you the power and coming of our Lord Jesus Christ, but we were eyewitnesses of his majesty."[7]

In all three cases, Paul, John, and Peter firmly place the story of redemption within a verifiable historical context. Theirs is not an argument framed from a philosophical point of view, nor is it one written to appeal to emotion, or to simply provide a basis for helping people find a hidden path toward a better life. Most emphatically not! Rather, it is an argument based on a historical reality. This man Jesus lived in history, died in history, and came back to life in history. Yes, there was a reason for his doing so, but without the verifiable reality of his life, death, and resurrection, none of that really matters.

John Stonestreet of the Colson Center, as he so often does, makes this same case in the context of a recent archeological find that confirms the existence of the biblical tribe of Edom. In an October 4, 2019, post he reminds us that,

> Unlike other religions, historical detail is central, even crucial to biblical faith. The biblical story reports on events that took place in actual human history. Unlike other religions, the protagonist of the biblical story is a God who has acted in the human arena, not in a mythical past or in another universe, but in the same setting as you, I, and everyone else who has ever lived.

> Since historical memory, and the actual acts of God within human history, is so central to biblical faith, we ought not be surprised when we find evidence of his activity in the ground.

> At the same time we should be ready to communicate the connections between history and faith when appropriate and when asked. [Just as Paul, Peter, and John did.] It's a wonderful way to communicate to our skeptical friends, family members, and coworkers what we believe and why we believe it.[8]

My point is simply this—if we want our students to live a life of genuine faith in an increasingly skeptical and defiant age, then we had better equip them with a reasonable faith based on something sound and sensible. What we believe to be true matters. Sincerity and fervency are important. They soon become impotent when cut off from reasonable and verifiable content. As J. P. Moreland argues, when our faith system is no longer held to be plausible within any historical or cultural context, people will jettison that system.[9] And that is exactly what is happening in the church today.

At the risk of sounding redundant—but then perhaps it is time to be a bit redundant—the reason behind much of the hand-wringing in the church over the tsunami of defections from the evangelical church, while complicated, can at least in part be based on the reality that fewer and fewer people in the church can actually give a reasoned, thoughtful, biblically sound defense for their faith. Too many who try—and most don't even try—get chewed up and then silently slip out of the side door of the church.

Christian Smith discovered this very thing in his extensive research on the spiritual and religious lives of American teenagers. Please pay careful attention to what he observed during his research. "Most teenagers talk about friends, school, sports, television, music, movies, romantic interests, family relationships, dealing with issues of drugs and alcohol, various organized activities with which they are involved, and specific fun or formative events they have experienced. What rarely rises in such conversations are teens' religious identities, beliefs, experiences, or practices. Religion just does not naturally seem to appear much on most teenagers' open-ended lists of what really matters in their lives. This is not surprising. It simply reflects the fact that there is very little built-in religious content or connection in the structure of most U.S. adolescents' daily schedule and routines."[10]

Instead, Smith notes, "Most U.S. teenagers' lives are dominated by school and homework; many are involved in sports and other clubs besides. Most teens spend lots of time with their friends just hanging out or doing things like going to the mall or bowling. In addition, most teens devote a great deal of life to watching television and movies, emailing or instant messaging friends, listening to music, and consuming other electronic media. Boyfriends and girlfriends sometimes consume a lot of teenage time and attention as well."[11]

He then goes on to make what should be an unsurprising observation. "We found very few teens from any religious background who are able to articulate well their religious beliefs and explain how those beliefs connect to the rest of their lives."[12]

If you are a parent or a pastor who takes your disciple-making responsibility seriously, that research-based statement should trouble you—deeply, in fact. At the very least it should cause you to wonder about the realities that underlie that conclusion from one of America's premier sociologists. None of this is surprising. As Dr. Smith says, "It simply reflects the fact that there is very little built-in content or connection in the structure of most U.S. adolescents' daily schedule and routine."[13]

Now, ask yourself why there is very little built-in content or connection in the structure of most U.S. adolescents' daily schedule and routine. With just a few seconds of reflection the answer will become obvious, at least obvious to anyone who is willing to be honest. Given where the vast majority of our kids attend school, there is no structure by which they can be immersed in a world of faith and learning. Thus, they are left largely defenseless against the crushing power of a predominantly secular cultural and educational establishment.

Yes, there is more to the discipling process than content, and I will make that clear in what follows. Without a solid foundation, however, everything eventually collapses. We've got to equip our young people so that they are, as Peter says, "prepared to make a defense to anyone who asks you for a reason for the hope that is in you."[14] It is important to note that Peter's admonition is given to those who are living in a hostile environment, who have been maligned and mistreated. Sound familiar?

One final note on this thread. Too often, Christian school leaders have engaged in an inappropriate and, in the end, ineffective approach to teaching content. We have done to our students what has become the current approach in the secular publicly funded school down the street. We have used more of an indoctrination approach to teaching faith content rather than engaging our students in a conversation about faith. Real-life engagement, the approach used by our Lord in His interactions with both His detractors and His disciples, is the best way to produce real-life faith.

Consider how often instead of dispensing content Jesus chooses to ask questions. His approach was actually consistent with how the rabbis of His day taught. It was also much like the Socratic method of inquiry that was and is central to a classical approach to teaching and learning. We see echoes of that in the project-oriented approach currently finding favor among many educators.

It is, I must say, about time. Say with me, "The sage on the stage is dead (or should be); the guide along the path is alive (or should be)." The guide will find it hard to lead in a direction about which he or she has no knowledge, however. That is why ensuring that your child has a capable guide is so crucial, especially when it comes to how we weave what we believe into the world in which we live.

As all of us know and have experienced, the joy of learning is not primarily found in just hearing content. It is only when a student actually experiences truth that he or she can fully grasp and embrace that truth, whether the topic is mathematics, science, geography, literature, or the gospel.

Content is crucial; however, on its own it is not enough. There must be more than a reasonable faith if our children, young people, and even our adults are to survive contact with reality. That is why there are more threads to explore.

## Third Thread: An Integrated Faith

It is never enough to just know. We must also understand and then act on what we know to be true. Failure to integrate what we know into how we live is one of the primary reasons why the church is making such little impact on the world around us.

Robert Lewis is one of many who have made this observation. Pay careful attention to what he has to say.

This is why we are not spanning the chasm and connecting with the community. We are trying to build bridges on truth alone, while the world around us is crying out for proof. Proof!

Our design is wrong. We need bridges that balance public proclamation with congregational incarnation. Bridges that are suspended by the steel cables of the Great Commandments as well as the Great Commission. In the twenty-first century the church must understand, as never before, that faith—without works—is dead. So too, will be our influence.

We do not, as many think, live in an age that despises belief. Rather, it is an age that wants to believe, desperately so. Deeply disillusioned by the failure of human reason and logic, it is open to outside—even supernatural—explanations. But it trusts nothing except what it can see and, more importantly, experience.

For the watching world, drowning in postmodernism, this is foundational: not simply the Word of Truth, but the Word made flesh. A living proof—an irrefutable incarnation.[15]

Many years ago, I stumbled across an article in *Moody Monthly* written by Irving Jensen, who at that time was the head of the Bible department at Bryan College in Dayton, Tennessee. It was the title to that article that captured my immediate attention: "Are We Training Athletes or Fattening Geese?" His premise was simple: When teaching the Bible, we spend way too much time communicating content and way too little time asking what we should do with what we are learning.

His question reflects the differences between how the Greeks and the Jews viewed teaching and learning. To the Greeks, an educated person was one who possessed the appropriate content. Knowledge for knowledge's sake was the goal. To a Jew, you were not educated until you could demonstrate in real-life scenarios what you claimed to know.

It's the difference between how we educate lawyers and doctors. To graduate from law school, you must show that you "know" the right content. You do that by passing the bar exam. Pass the exam and you are licensed to practice law. As a student who studies medicine, you must also demonstrate that you "know" the pertinent content. You don't get to practice medicine, however, until you've done an internship during which you demonstrate that you know what to do with the content you've accumulated over the years.

Seminaries, by the way, function a lot more like law schools than medical schools. There has been some movement away from content-only approaches, but not nearly enough. It is interesting to note that a seminary degree is not one of the qualifications for eldership that Paul lists in his letter to Timothy.[16] A life of faith or leadership is not based on what you know alone. If what you know doesn't shape how you behave, then you have given everyone the right to question your faith.[17]

The apostle John makes this clear when he writes, "For this is the message that you have heard from the beginning, that we should love one another." That is the content piece. He then goes on to share a crucial truth that must express itself in our actions. "By this we know love, that he laid down his life for us, and we ought to lay down our lives for the brothers." Now ponder what the apostle whom Jesus loved says next. "But if anyone has the world's goods and sees his brother in need, yet closes his heart against him, how does God's love abide in him? Little children, let us not love in word or talk, but in deed and truth."[18]

Now we can, and should, think and even argue about how best to fulfill this expectation. We may not always agree on the best way to help people in a manner that most accurately demonstrates the reality of God's love. We are not, however, given a pass. We are not allowed to say, "Well, that's an interesting fact" and then move on with life as usual. We are expected to act on what we know. Failure to do so is an act of disobedience and a demonstration that we don't fully understand what it means to love Christ as a true disciple should.

For those engaged in Christian schooling to ignore this crucial truth is to call into question the entirety of our enterprise, and rightfully so. This is another one of the common criticisms I hear from church leaders about their local Christian school. They just don't see the fruit of the Spirit in those students. They don't see genuine evidence of all of the content that we are pouring into their minds. Thus, Irving Jensen's question—are we training athletes or fattening geese?—is important. In one sense it is a one-question quiz that we seem to fail time and time again.

We would never do something similar with our athletic teams or fine arts programs. We would never be satisfied that our football players could explain a particular offensive or defensive scheme. Until they can go onto the field and execute that particular scheme, and do so with excellence, no coach would be satisfied. The same could be said of any drama, vocal, or instrumental presentation. Getting the script or score right without also delivering the heart and "guts" of any drama or musical performance would be unacceptable to any director.

So it must be for those of us engaged in Christian schooling. We've got to do more than just get the facts right. We've got to help our students wrestle through the implications of those facts and then encourage them to find ways to bring those truths to life in a broken world so desperate for living proof that what we say is true, that our content is true. And by the way, we as adults can't fulfill that responsibility, as I will show, until we ourselves have acted wisely and well on what we know to be true.

By the way, that is exactly what God did when He sent His Son into our world. Without the incarnation, we would never know God as we do. It is one of the primary reasons Jesus came to earth. It is why He said, "If you have seen me, you have seen the Father." It wasn't just an affirmation that the Son and the Father are equal. That is certainly true. But there is more. The Son was an absolutely accurate reflection of the Father's nature, character, and qualities.

It has been left to us to carry on that mission. The final apologetic, as Francis Schaeffer reminded us, is not our ability to rattle off theological pieties. Rather, it is our ability to reflect in our lives and interactions with people the very image of the One we claim to embrace as our Lord. Failure to help our children and young people understand and act on that reality invalidates all of our efforts.

There is a further truth here that each of us engaged in this thing called Christian schooling must understand and embrace, something key in understanding the incarnation. It is this. For people to believe what we have to say not only requires a living proof of faith; it also requires a faithful guide, someone who clearly and very personally embodies the faith that they proclaim. That reality is another reason why Christian schooling is so essential to the mission of making disciples.

## Fourth Thread: An Embodied Faith

I've often spoken of the remarkable impact the people at New Testament Baptist Church and Dade Christian School had on my life. As I look back on those years, I am struck by the number of people who took part in shaping my life and what I came to believe was true. More on that concept in the next chapter. For now, I want to make this observation. I came to believe what I believed and came to behave as I behaved less because of what I learned formally in Sunday school, worship services, or the classroom and more because of what I observed.

Yes, the formal teaching piece was important. Remember, however, that the heart of my argument goes like this: Unless all of the threads I am in the process of identifying are woven together into a whole piece, then we are unlikely to achieve the real goals of Christian schooling.

For example, I remember with great fondness Julian Gunter, who served as my Sunday school teacher during my freshman year of high school. Julian was a big man, a former college football player, the proverbial gentle giant—except on the football field. What I remember most was not, however, his size or athletic prowess. What caught my attention, even as a hurting kid, was the clear fact that he was an incarnation of what he taught us about the person of Jesus Christ. His was a life of integrity. And I observed most of that outside of that small room where we met on Sunday mornings.

Julian was the one who introduced me to the game of golf, and not just to me but to all of the guys in our class. Not everyone took to the game, but for those who did, Julian took the opportunity to teach us how to behave on the golf course. No club throwing and definitely no use of problematic language. He taught us to be gentlemen in every sense of the word because, as he reminded us often, we were ambassadors of Christ, representatives of Him to a dark and broken world. "Never let your behavior cast a poor reflection on your Savior," he would often say to us.

We also did some camping and fishing that year, which for all of us guys was a lot of fun. And while we caught a lot of fish—which is easy to do in the Florida Keys—it wasn't about the fish; it was about the conversation around the campfire in the evenings. As with golf, Julian taught us how to care for God's creation because, well, because it belonged to God and we were called to be stewards of this great gift. I guess he was an original conservationist, but one who understood that it wasn't about Mother Nature but rather about the Creator.

Julian Gunter was a powerful influence in my life not because he invited us to do some fun things. That was part of it, of course. The real power was not in golf or fishing. It was in observing a life that was consistent no matter where we were, whether in a Sunday school room or on a boat in the Keys. It was that consistency, that wholeness, that integrity that made the impression on the mind and heart of this struggling kid.

Steven Garber gives us a good definition of that word *integrity*. For him integrity occurs when what you say you believe in your heart actually shapes how you behave in public.[19] That idea is actually very much akin to how Patrick Lencioni describes a healthy organization. He writes, "An organization has integrity—is healthy—when it is whole, consistent, and complete, that is, when its management, operations, strategy and culture fit together and make sense."[20] That means that as school leaders, one of our primary responsibilities is to ensure that every action by every person is aligned with what we say is true of the organization we represent.

It's a biblical concept that gets too little attention. It's at the heart of Jesus' condemnation of the scribes and Pharisees. "The scribes and the Pharisees," Jesus observes, "sit on Moses' seat, so do and observe whatever they tell you, but not the works they do. For they preach, but do not practice."[21] In the life of Jesus, however, we see none of that. His actions were always fully aligned with His Father's purposes and fully reflective of His Father's nature and character. As imperfect as our efforts may be, that should always be our goal as well.

Whether organizationally or individually, here is a key piece of reality. No one can trust anything you say if they don't see congruence between your words and your actions. I trusted Julian Gunter because there was not the slightest variation between his words and his actions. He was a man who truly embodied God's Word. So must all of us who claim a call from Christ to engage in the hugely important work of Christian schooling.

It was a lesson I rediscovered quite quickly but in an unexpected way during my first years teaching in a Christian high school. I was just a kid, only twenty-three, when I started teaching high school. I had thirty-seven students in my first American history class (only thirty-five or so textbooks, but that is another story). I loved teaching to a large extent because I loved my students. I discovered, though, that I could reach some kids easier than others. Why was that, I often wondered? Was it me? And of course, as teachers, we do discover that we will typically resonate with some of our students more than others. There was more to this, however, than just variations in personality.

In those days at Hollywood Christian School, we were required to make a visit to each home of each student in our homeroom at least once during the year. (Try that as a requirement at your school today!) Fortunately, I was the senior-class sponsor, and there were fewer than thirty students for whom I was "responsible." It was still a lot of work, but it was work that bore enormous fruit over the course of the year.

As I got to know the students and parents, I discovered something interesting. Over time I divided my students into three groups. There were the kids who came from great homes, homes where the parents lived lives of integrity. There were kids who came from broken, openly dysfunctional families—we had an open enrollment policy. And there were kids who came from "church families," but families where there was a definite lack of alignment with true faith.

Guess which of groups of students became my greatest challenge? I'll give you a clue. It wasn't the kids from the dysfunctional, nonbelieving homes. In almost every case it was the kids from the families where there was an external commitment to faith but a definite lack of integrity. I soon came to understand the attitude of those kids. They just assumed I was like mom and dad, that my faith was superficial and not life-altering. Sadly, there is a lot of that going around, and not just with parents.

I am going to say this as graciously as I can, though I'm not sure that there is a gracious way of saying this. Any head of school who tolerates a lack of integrity in the life of any teacher has failed at his or her most fundamental responsibility. In so doing we misrepresent the very One who gave Himself on our behalf and on whose behalf we are called to service. And in the end, we discredit the mission to which we have been called.

Here, however, is a key to why Christian schooling matters. In Christian schooling, no matter what form it takes, we have the freedom to make tough decisions about who gets to teach and thus impact our children. Try that at your local secular public school.

## Content, Action, and Incarnation

Most of us understand that schooling is very much about content. There are things that our students need to know: how to read, how to compose a cogent paragraph, how to view the world in which we live, its significant events, current challenges, and our role in what is and what might lie ahead. We want our students to understand the building blocks of nature and the universe, to grasp the ideas and arguments of influential people, and to appreciate the contributions of those who have given us great art and literature. It is a noble calling.

With a little thought and personal reflection, we also come to understand that people always grasp more fully what they experience; that content alone is a poor substitute for touching, tasting, creating, tearing apart something with our own hands, or creating something with what we are learning.

Finally, I would ask you to close your eyes, to shut out the world's intrusions for just a moment, and ponder this simple question: Which of your teachers made a huge impact on your life? I suspect that a face, or hopefully several, will soon come to mind. I also suspect that when you stop to consider why that teacher had such a positive impact in your life, you will arrive at a simple conclusion. In that teacher there was a wonderful, remarkable combination of factors.

They knew their stuff. They had the content down cold. They made it all come to life and showed how that stuff could and should make a difference in life. And finally, they weren't just talking heads spewing out data and factoids. When they taught you sensed that all of this came from not just their head but from their heart as well, indeed from the very core of their life. They were what they said. Here was a whole person, a person of absolute integrity. Be that kind of teacher and you may not change the world, but you will change the life of some student some time.

A final question to parents and pastors reading this book. Isn't that what you want for your children? Isn't that what you want for the members of the flock over which you have been given a shepherding and discipling responsibility? I hope so. If so, there's nothing wrong in demanding that from those who lead the school where your child attends or from those who teach the classes in which your child receives instruction. Integrity is key. Don't ever surrender that for any reason.

## For Reflection

1. Be honest. What beliefs and experiences shape your understanding of the purpose of education? Upon what are those beliefs based?

2. In your mind, what is the difference between indoctrination and inquiry? Is it a bad idea to allow students to ask tough questions? Why or why not?

3. Can anyone really "know" something without putting that knowledge into practice? What is the danger if we never, for example, put faith into everyday practice? Consider James 1:22–26, 2:14–26 and 1 John 3:16–18 in answering this question.

4. Have you had a Julian Gunter in your life? How many? If so, how did they influence you?

5. Do your children have enough of those kinds of influencers in their lives? If not, what can you do to increase the possible influence of those kinds of people?

Chapter 7

## The Final Threads

I've seen it far too many times than I care to recall. So, I suspect, have you. And it's heartbreaking every time. Let me illustrate with a story.

Scott and Rachel were two of my favorite students. Rachel, a year older, was an exceptional student, insightful and diligent and possessed of a great sense of humor. Scott too was an exceptional student, but he was also a great athlete, a three-sport letterman in the days when that was still possible. Their parents became, especially to my wife, important mentors who helped us navigate the early years of our marriage. While not perfect, they were certainly committed to following and serving Christ. It was the kind of home we would wish for all of our students.

There was a third child, Evan. He was the youngest, and truth be told, the most talented of the group. It wasn't his prowess in the classroom or on the football field that set him apart. He just had that quality that made people like him, call it charisma or charm or whatever, but he never wanted for friends. He did have a beautiful singing voice that he worked hard to develop and which eventually formed the basis of his career.

Sadly, Evan chose a path that took him far from his family and faith. He made choices more informed by popular culture than by Christ. As David unpacks for us in Psalm 1, Evan chose to walk the path that leads to death—in his case, literally—and broke his parents' and siblings' hearts in the process.

So, here's the question. Why do some kids, in spite of all kinds of advantages, go off the rails? It's a question we've asked and with which we have struggled since Cain rejected God's way and murdered his brother, Abel. Like you, I have labored often to find an adequate answer to that question. I assumed for years that discovery of such an answer would allow me to formulate a plan to reverse that kind of tragic end.

Here's what I have discovered. There is no plan. There is no formula that once employed will reverse the course that some people choose to take in life. There is, of course, the Holy Spirit, who sometimes invades the heart in such a way that an entire life is changed dramatically. I saw that in the life of my own brother. His return to faith after years of wandering was a joyous time much like what we read about in Jesus' story of the prodigal son. Just as often, however, people continue to travel the troubled road of death.

Why is that the case? I'm not sure that I have an answer for that. It's kind of like the whole conversation about the place where God's sovereignty and man's responsibility meet. We all know there is an intersection of the two, but we aren't always sure about how all of that works out in reality. That mystery may fascinate us or frustrate us, but we've still got to figure out how to keep from being paralyzed when facing such a situation. Because this is such a dilemma, I long ago decided to add the next thread to my formula for weaving the fabric of faithfulness.

## Fifth Thread: A Willing Faith

God gives us commandments. The Scriptures are filled with things we are to do and things we are to avoid. As has often been noted, God didn't send Moses down from the mountain with the Ten Suggestions. Rather He gave us the Ten Commandments, ten clear concepts around which faithful followers of Yahweh and His Son must—must— shape their lives.

When the Pharisees asked Jesus the question, "What is the greatest of the commandments?" He didn't hesitate in His response. "Love the Lord your God with all of your heart, soul, and mind. And the second is like the first, "Love your neighbor as yourself."[1] It's what we are called to do. It's what we are instructed to do. It's what's expected of us. It is a command, not a mere recommendation.

Like any command, however, we have choices. We can obey, we can distort what appears to be plain, or we can simply choose to disobey. It happens all the time, every day, all around the world. It's why we have penalties attached to decisions to violate the law.

What intrigues me about this reality is that God never forces His will on anyone. He never says, "You must." It's always, "You should." However we understand the concept of free will, the fact remains that we do have the choice to obey God's commands or to say, "I'm not really interested, thank you."

If we are honest with ourselves, we've all been at that point sometime in our lives, probably multiple times. And if we are equally honest, we have all experienced the prompting of the Holy Spirit, the clear teaching of the Scriptures, the pressure of our surrounding community, or our personal experiences, that the Holy Spirit uses to move us in the direction of obedience—at least most of the time.

Sometimes, and for some people most of the time, we choose a contrary path for reasons that might puzzle and confound those around us. We see it nearly every day in our families, in our churches, in our schools. While there are usually more Scotts and Rachels, there will always be the Evans as well. So what do we do, and how does that shape the formation of our fabric?

## It Just Is

One of my favorite insights from Steven Garber's *The Fabric of Faithfulness* is the following observation: "One thing is clear: for those who learn the deepest lessons—ones in which visions of one's world and one's place in it are transformed—there is always a teacher whose purposes and passions ignite a student's moral imagination."[2]

Sit and ponder that thought a bit. Then, if you are a teacher, be encouraged that your efforts are not in vain. The possibility of life transformation is a reality, and your role in those efforts will not be futile. You can and do make a difference every day, whether you see the immediate impact or not.

Garber then goes on to say something a bit less heartening. "But it is also clear that, in the end, it is the students who choose to learn from their teachers who experience this metamorphosis of moral meaning."[3] There it is. There is the difficult reality. We can do everything right. We can pour our lives into our students. We can encourage, we can cajole, we can nurture, we can seek to inspire, we can do all within our power. What we can't do is decide on behalf of any student. They must make the call. We see this in the anguished words of our Lord as He walks away from another confrontation with the Pharisees. "O Jerusalem, Jerusalem, the city that kills the prophets and stones those who are sent to it! How often would I have gathered your children together as a hen gathers her brood under her wings, and you were not willing!"[4]

Breaking His heart even more was the knowledge of where all of this rejection and disobedience would eventually lead. "See, your house is left desolate," He cries out.[5] Jesus knew that in just a few brief years Jerusalem would lie in ruins and the people of Israel would be scattered throughout the world, hated and despised wherever they went. Yet, even the Son of God could not "make" people do the right thing. Nor can you.

At this moment, permit me a word about one of the most misused and misunderstood verses in the Old Testament. You've heard it quoted innumerable times, and so have I. In fact, you may have used it yourself. It goes like this in the old King James, "Train up a child in the way he should go and when he is old he will not depart from it."[6]

There are two huge problems with how we typically choose to explain that text. Derek Kidner helps us with the first. "The training prescribed is literally, 'according to his (the child's) way,' implying, it seems, respect for his individuality and vocation, though not for his self-will."[7] The training they are to receive should be based on the truth of God's Word, certainly. The meaning of "the way he should go," however, refers more to the way they have been wired, to their interests and gifting, rather than to specific steps they should take. It refers more to the idea of an individual education plan than to an ultimate way of life. We would desire that each child see the world through a sound biblical lens, but we should also desire that they see how they can live fully for Christ in the unique manner which they have been created.

The second problem is more fundamental and has to do with understanding the rules we need to apply when interpreting any Scripture. For example, we should approach a historical text like the book of Acts differently than we would approach a didactic text like the Pauline letters or how we would interpret poetic portions of the Bible such as the Psalms. Thus, when we read the Proverbs, we need to understand that there are considerations that must shape our reading of those wonderful words of wisdom.

For example, proverbs are not laws in the same sense as the Levitical laws or the Ten Commandments. They are also not promises, but words of wisdom that provide us insight into the probabilities of what is likely to happen if we take those words to heart.

For example, a person who lives a righteous life is more likely to live into old age. That is not, however, a promise. We all know, either personally or through history, a lot of very godly people who died at a young age. Would anyone suggest that God didn't keep His promise to those people? I suspect some people just might make that observation. The truth is that God does keep His promises. Long life is just not a promise He has made to us. Live righteously, work diligently, make wise decisions, don't abuse your body, and don't fall prey to disease or fatal injury, and the more probable outcome will be long life.

People who cling to Proverbs 22:6 as a promise often end up feeling huge levels of guilt when a child goes down the wrong path. They ask, "Where did I go wrong?" "What could I have done differently?" "Why is God punishing me with this?" Perhaps that person could have done something different. Whether it would have made any difference is unknowable. What we do know is that sometimes, some people exercise their free will to choose the wrong path. That is one of the sad realities of life.

## So, What Do We Do?

Isn't that the question? Doesn't it haunt you as much as it did our Lord? If you lead a Christian school, how many times has someone accused you of just giving up on a student who has been given not only a second chance but often a third, fourth, or fifth chance? Don't you have any compassion, they ask? Where's your understanding of grace? Isn't this a "Christian" school? How can you abandon this kid? You have, I am sure, heard it all multiple times. The questions hurt, and your failure to see a kid make the right choice pierces your heart. So, what do you do?

Here are some brief thoughts I'd ask you to consider.

- Start by repeating after me: "Sometimes people just choose to make bad choices in spite of all we try to do on their behalf." Remember it was not one of the Sanhedrin who betrayed Jesus. It was Judas, one of the twelve. So, are we supposed to ask, "What did Jesus do wrong?" Of course not. We know He didn't do anything wrong, yet Judas did the unthinkable. He betrayed his teacher, his friend, his Lord.
- Acknowledge that sometimes we do "provoke" children to wrath by our decisions and actions. We could engage in a pretty healthy debate over the meaning of legalism, and we might come to some differing conclusions. I can say one thing with confidence, however. Legalism kills the soul. Life transformation is beyond the capacity of the law. If you persist in the belief that your efforts to control every aspect of your students' lives will produce godliness, you will forever be disappointed.
- Does that mean that we do away with rules? Of course not. It does mean that these questions should be asked of every rule. Does this rule . . .
  1. Help cultivate a love for God and for those around us—in the school and in the surrounding community? In other words, does it force us to consider the Great Commandments to love God and to love our neighbors as ourselves?

2. Reflect the nature and character of God? And if so, can we clearly show how the two are related to one another?
3. Advance the purposes of Christ in our school and in the world at large?
4. Allow our students to better focus on and understand what is beautiful, what is good, and what is true?
5. Encourage our students to achieve excellence in all they do?
6. Foster healthy relationships and what the Marine Corps calls esprit de corps? In other words, does it make for a healthier culture at your school?

These are suggestions. You should have this kind of conversation with your board, your leadership team, your faculty, and your parents.

- Remember: There is always a teacher. To ask students to just figure it out on their own is an unlikely way to achieve your desired goal. All of us need a Moses or a Joshua or a Barnabas or a Paul or an Aquilla or a Priscilla; we all need a mentor or a coach. Here is the simple fact: You, as a teacher or a parent, can't do it alone, nor can your students. It is never enough to point a kid in the right direction. You've got to give him or her a guide. To expel a student from your school having failed to give them that kind of resource is unacceptable. By the way, that mentor may be a local pastor or perhaps a retired businessman or woman, or even a local college student who has been down the same road. It doesn't necessarily need to be a teacher or coach, though it could be.
- Don't expect every student to embrace what you teach. Do expect every student to take up the responsibility to live in peace with what fellow students and faculty believe to be true. Doing so demonstrates respect. We learn that from Daniel's life. He certainly never adopted the pagan gods of Babylon or Persia, but he always acted with profound respect toward those around him.
- Remove the student without hesitation when it becomes apparent to you and to his or her mentor that they have no intention of diverting from their destructive path. When the doctor says, "You've got a tumor," you don't hesitate, not if you are wise. You cut it out or you kill it. The consequences are too severe to your body to do otherwise. That is why the apostle Paul tells us with certainty that "Bad company corrupts good morals."[8]

Making the potentially life-changing decision to remove a student from your school community is one of the most painful decisions any school leader will ever make. It is, however, a sad necessity at times. You will never be able to help a student fashion the fabric of faithfulness without that student's willing participation in the process.

## Sixth Thread: A Community Faith

We live at a time and in a place where our perception of community and its importance is at a low ebb. As a consequence, we have lost a key understanding as to how our thinking and character are best shaped.

Consider this insight from sociologist Robert Bellah: "There are truths we do not see when we adopt the language of radical individualism. We find ourselves, not independently of other people and institutions, but through them. We never get to the bottom of ourselves on our own. We discover who we are face-to-face, side-by-side with others in work, love, and learning. . . . We are part of a larger whole that we can neither forget nor imagine in our own image without paying a high price."[9]

I find it fascinating that when Jesus called His disciples, He called them to a community. And when He sent them out on a mission, He never sent them alone. He always sent them as teams, who then returned to the community for what we today would call a debrief. It's how we best learn. There are a ton of implications for how we approach teaching and learning in that reality.

I practice that concept whenever I lead a school through a strategic planning process. I pull together a large group of people who more than likely hold different perspectives, experiences, and insights for the purpose of engaging in some rather important conversations about a school's future. I have found that in those differing outlooks the way forward is most often found.

It is, by the way, exactly how Christ designed the church. We are a body made up of many members, all of whom have been sovereignly given diverse sets of gifts by the Holy Spirit. Thus, the apostle Paul directs us to a vital truth when he observes, "The eye cannot say to the hand, 'I have no need of you,' nor again the head to the feet, 'I have no need of you.'"[10] It's this simple. We need one another. We cannot function without one another. And as Bellah points out, "We discover who we are face-to-face, side-by-side with others in life, love, and learning."[11]

The clearest biblical example of that is, I believe, to be found in the New Testament book of Hebrews. In one sense the following portion of that book is a pretty good summary of much of what I have been saying over the last three chapters of this book. Beginning in 10:23 we read, "Let us hold fast the confession of our faith without wavering, for he who promised is faithful [there's that reasonable faith piece]. And let us consider how to stir up one another to love and good works [there are those integrated and incarnational pieces], not neglecting to meet together, as is the habit of some [there's the community piece], but encouraging one another, and all the more as you see the Day drawing near [there's the urgency of what we are called to do].[12]

I suspect some will respond with, "Well Dr. Pue, the text is clearly talking about the *church*, not about school." To which I will reply, "So what!" The word *church* as used in the New Testament does not refer to the same type of reality we find in most evangelical congregations. Look at the instruction, encouragement, and exhortation found in the New Testament epistles. The effort required to make disciples requires a level of intentionality, intensiveness, and just plain rubbing shoulders with one another that simply can't be reproduced in a one-hour-a-week class. Discipleship is intended to be a whole-life, full-time process.

I can't imagine (perhaps you can) why anyone would think it a bad thing to intentionally and intensively immerse our children and young people daily in a place where they will be taught what is good, what is beautiful, and what is true. Where they will be surrounded with teachers who seek to be an incarnation of Christ in all they do. Where they will be encouraged and challenged to ponder every aspect of the world and their role in that world through the eyes of the Creator.

So, remind me again, how can that be a bad thing? What actually stuns me, however, is that there are people who actually believe that exposing our kids to a barrage of false and faulty thinking on a daily basis is a good idea. I have tried thus far in this book to argue passionately, and hopefully persuasively, that the Scriptures make clear that such an approach to education is a bad thing, to be avoided at all costs.

Sadly, the very understanding of community, what it is, how it functions, and why it is critical, is unraveling. There are lots of reasons for what is happening. We, as Americans, have long been in love with the idea of the rugged individualist. We see that theme running through much of our literature and social mythology, from stories of Wild West cowboys to the up-by-the-bootstrap stories of self-made millionaires (now billionaires).

In reality, America has seldom been about that towering individual. While it is true that the American system has allowed for people to accomplish extraordinary things not possible in much of the world, the real truth about America's strength is to be found in what are called mediating structures: our churches, our civic organizations, and our families.

As this is not a book primarily about community, I will not delve deeper into the idea, but here is one final thought. Technology is most certainly a two-edged sword. On one side it makes our life easier and simpler. On the other side it tends to both shape culture through its powerful and ubiquitous presence and to exacerbate the worst impulses of individuals within that culture. We ignore that reality to our peril.

Dr. Sherry Turkle is a faculty member at the Massachusetts Institute of Technology, one of America's most prestigious universities. She was hired at MIT as a sociologist and psychologist to study the impact of technology on individuals and communities. She is no closet "luddite," but a thoughtful, exceptional researcher. If community is an essential thread in the creation of the fabric of faithfulness, I believe we should pay careful attention to conclusions to which her research has led her.

> But we have come to a point at which it is near heresy to suggest that MySpace or Facebook or Second Life is not community. I have used the word community myself and argued that these environments correspond to what sociologist Ray Oldenberg called 'the great good place.' These were the coffee shops, the parks, and the barbershops that used to be points of assembly for acquaintances and neighbors, the people who made up the landscape of life.

> I think I spoke too quickly. I used the word 'community' for worlds of weak ties. Communities are constituted by physical proximity, shared concerns, real consequences, and common responsibilities. Its members help each other in the most practical ways . . . in community families take care of each other, help each other when money is tight, where there is illness, when someone dies. If one family is evicted it boarders with a neighboring one. They bury each other. Now here comes the key reality. "What do we owe one another in simulation?"[13]

I know all about GoFundMe pages, but that cold reality misses the point, an important point, of what it means to be committed to one another. It is a pale imitation of community. It is the difference between sending your money to help fund a relief effort and getting on a plane or in a car to head into the heat of battle. And that difference is profound. Our kids deserve to see community in action.

They need to see faith integrated into the hard, often painful realities of life, not just while sitting in their climate-controlled classrooms. They need to see faith embodied daily in the lives of the people who have embraced the call to serve as teachers, coaches, and mentors. Only in so doing can our children and young people have any hope of seeing faith that doesn't flinch from encounters with the messy realities of life. And they will experience that more fully, as Bellah suggests, face-to-face, side-by-side, and as Turkle encourages, not virtual but real.

Remember, Satan is like a roaring lion, roaming the countryside looking for someone to devour. And like a lion he is always looking for the straggler because a lost, displaced animal simply makes an easier target. Dietrich Bonhoeffer often spoke of this challenge. "Let him who cannot be alone beware of community . . . Let him who is not in community beware of being alone . . . Each by itself has profound perils and pitfalls. One who wants fellowship without solitude plunges into the void of words and feelings, and the one who seeks solitude without fellowship perishes in the abyss of vanity, self-infatuation, and despair."[14]

Your kids can't fight this battle alone. The enemy is too shrewd, too powerful. They need a healthy community to surround them, to encourage them, and yes, at times to protect them.

Here is a simple fact that every pastor and parent should consider: Schooling is simply a means by which the church is better able to fulfill its call to make disciples by extending its reach beyond a limited hour or two a week and by helping students better see how the Scriptures touch on every sphere of life. That it takes place in the kind of community envisioned in Scripture simply gives greater power to its efforts and, according to the research, leads to far better outcomes.

## Seventh Thread: A Consuming Faith

We all know the story of Saul's encounter with Christ on the road to Damascus. It was a pretty dramatic moment and one that literally changed the world.[15] Do a little bit of research and you will discover how often something similar has changed the course of a life and often of an entire people.

The image, however, of falling to your knees in fear is not one the church likes to elevate in this current age. We would rather talk about how God loves you and has a wonderful plan for your life. It is true, of course, that God loves you, and he does have a plan for your life—wonderful, however, might depend on your definition of the word *wonderful*. As the author of the New Testament book of Hebrews reminds us, things don't always turn out well for even the most ardent, faithful followers of God.

"And what more shall I say? For time would fail me to tell of Gideon, Barak, Samson, Jephthah, of David and Samuel and the prophets—who through faith conquered kingdoms, enforced justice, obtained promises, stopped the mouths of lions, quenched the power of fire, escaped the edge of the sword, were made strong out of weakness, became mighty in war, put foreign armies to flight." So far so good, right?

But then he goes on to say, "Some were tortured, refusing to accept release, so that they might rise again to a better life. Others suffered mocking and flogging, and even chains and imprisonment. They were stoned, they were drawn in two, they were killed with the sword. They went about in skins of sheep and goats, destitute, afflicted, mistreated—of whom the world is not worthy—wandering in deserts and mountains and dens and caves of the earth."

Now here is the summary, the key to what it often means to live life as a sojourner, as an alien (think of all those people seeking to cross our southern border). "And all of these, though commended through their faith, did not receive what was promised, since God had provided something better for us."[16]

Sometimes, as the saying goes, the journey of a thousand miles ends badly. So, the obvious question is this: Why in the world would we ever start on a journey that might just end badly in the here and now? The answer to that question is actually quite simple, one that this same author answers a bit earlier in chapter 11. "These all died in faith, not having received the things promised, but having seen them and greeted them from afar, and having acknowledged that they were strangers and exiles on the earth. For people who speak thus make it clear that they are seeking a homeland. If they had been thinking of that land from which they had gone out, they would have had opportunity to return."

Now here is the key. "But as it is, they desire a better country, that is a heavenly one. Therefore God is not ashamed to be called their God, for he has prepared for them a city."[17]

Two quick thoughts. First, we are not called to live as though our actions have no impact on our current reality, within our current culture. We have an obligation for the here-and-now because we are called to be stewards of God's grace wherever we may find ourselves at any time in history. As representatives, literally ambassadors, we simply cannot retreat from that obligation without bringing dishonor to our Lord.

Second, like it or not, as followers of Jesus Christ we will sometimes find ourselves on the wrong side of cultural norms. We are actually seeing some of that reality in our country today. For most followers of Jesus Christ, for most of history, cultural conflict has been the norm. Thus, to take up our cross—a symbol of shame—to follow Him requires a level of courage and grit that can't be enforced well externally. Each follower of Jesus Christ must make that decision on his or her own. It's why a willing faith is a crucial thread in creating the fabric of faithfulness. No one—no parent, pastor, or teacher—can live faith for their children.

That, in my mind, is why this thread, a consuming faith, is so essential. In fact, it is, I believe, the most essential of the threads. Without it the entire garment will most certainly unravel under the pressures of life. It's why Solomon places it as the key element in the drama he describes in Proverbs. It's what he (and David in the Psalms) calls the "fear of the Lord," and what he tells us is the absolute, essential ingredient in a life of faith.[18]

That word *fear*, as it is used by Solomon and David, is so often misunderstood. It simply means "a worshiping submission"[19] I say simply because it isn't hard to understand the real meaning of the word. Living that concept in our daily life is, however, anything but simple. It requires the willingness to die daily, as our Lord unhesitatingly instructs us to do.[20]

It also requires a huge amount of self-awareness and self-discipline, as the apostle Paul makes clear.[21] And it isn't something that we can do easily on our own, which is why we need the thread of community. It is difficult to live a fully robust life of faith if we don't possess a sound biblical basis for how best to live that kind of life in such a broken, fallen world. That foundation is what a reasonable faith provides for us. And all of that is made easier with guides who, by their life example and encouragement, help us along on what is often a challenging journey. Hopefully, you are beginning to get how all of these threads fit together in that web I am calling the fabric of faithfulness.

None of that will, however, take root until a person is willing to stand before God and say, "Yes!" Yes to His grace and love. Yes to His sovereign authority. Yes to His call to our place in His world. Yes to our responsibility to His creation and to all those who inhabit that creation.

And yes, while it is true that we need to constantly be renewing our mind as Paul instructs us in his letter to the Romans, we must first and foremost give God our heart. That is why Paul first calls us to present our bodies as a living sacrifice, which he describes as a necessary act of worship.[22] The mind without the heart becomes a cold, sterile place. The heart without the mind may run hot, but that heat too often leads to unhelpful, even destructive behavior. Insisting on both is what Jim Collins calls the genius of the AND.[23]

I close this chapter with a thought from James K. A. Smith, author of a profoundly important book, *Desiring the Kingdom*.

> It is usually understood that education is about ideas and information. And so distinctively Christian education is understood to be about Christian ideas. On this account, the goal of Christian education is the development of a Christian perspective, or more commonly now, a Christian worldview, which is taken to be a system of Christian beliefs, ideas, and doctrines.
>
> But what if this line of thinking is off on the wrong foot? What if education ... is not primarily about the absorption of ideas and information but about the formation of hearts and desires? What if we began appreciating how education not only gets in our heads, but also (and more fundamentally) grabs us by the gut—what the New Testament refers to as the heart?[24]

What if?

Now permit me to give you the briefest look ahead to two final and crucial pieces of my argument. First, I will be jumping into shark-infested waters, so to speak, as I seek to address the reluctance and even hostility expressed by many pastors and parents when engaged in any discussion about Christian schooling, especially when the conversation turns to Christian schools. It is astonishing, actually. I will look specifically at our own country because what is true here is most definitely not true in other parts of the world. In taking on the task of writing these next two chapters, I am aware that I am liable to alienate some people. It is a risk I must take, however, if I am to accurately represent what the Scriptures have to say about schooling.

Second, I believe it important to provide some historical background on how we have arrived at our current destination in regard to education in the USA. Far too many people believe that what we are doing today is just more of what we have always done. That is not true. What is true, however, is that historical events and cultural constructs have had far more influence on the means of education in our country than has the Word of God.

## For Reflection

1. Does the story of Evan encourage or discourage you? Why? Has a flawed understanding of Proverbs 22:6 shaped your thinking as a parent? In what ways?

2. So what do you do as a parent, as a pastor, as a teacher when a student chooses to disregard the Scriptures and your counsel? What can you do?

3. Why is "community" so important to our discipling and schooling efforts? Consider Robert Bellah's observations as you answer that question. Next, consider all that the New Testament has to say about the community called the church.

4. If the fear of God is the foundation of all that we do to disciple ourselves and our children, how must that shape our educational efforts?

5. Please read the quote from James K. A. Smith found at the end of this chapter and answer his question: What if?

Chapter 8

# Questions That Must Be Asked

In the Harry Potter stories the chief adversary is a wizard gone bad by the name of Voldemort. He is a persona of such power and malignant intent that people are reluctant to even mention his name. So, he is often referenced as "he who should not be named."

In that sense I often feel a bit like Voldemort—a quite startling statement, I am sure. Let me explain what I mean by making that comparison. It isn't that I see myself as a malign influence, and I certainly don't have any power. But on many occasions over the years, I have asked questions of the status quo that have put me on the "wrong" side of a number of issues. It isn't so much my name that should be kept silent. Rather, it is the questions I tend to raise that, in the opinion of many, should not be asked. It is better, some think, to just remain silent rather than risk the ire of those to whom I am posing my questions.

As my wife can well attest, I am not, however, willing to back away from issues that need to be addressed or questions that need to be asked; even when posing those questions or pursuing those issues can put me at risk. Now, I don't consider myself a particularly courageous person. Nor do I believe that my questions are simply the idiosyncratic musings of an unmoored mind. Rather I see them as necessary if we are to take seriously our responsibility to obediently and effectively fulfill our calling with wisdom, grace, and excellence. And as I've already hopefully made clear, our calling is simple: make disciples.

So, I am always a bit puzzled but not terribly surprised at Christians' responses when I step into the arena, as I have with this book, to call into question the church's grasp of and commitment to a genuine biblical understanding of disciple making—and how the everyday education of our children and young people fits as a strategy to achieve our singular task to "make disciples who obey all that I have taught you."

## Uncomfortable Questions

Here comes one of those questions that should not be uttered: Is it really our mission to make converts of all nations? Looking through the lens of history at the church's efforts throughout much of the last two thousand years might lead some to believe that to be the case. And let's be honest. It is quite a sexy (forgive my use of that word, but it conveys a truth) and compelling message in a fundraising context to speak of all the thousands of people who make a profession of faith through our efforts. Certainly we should desire to see people come to faith in Christ.

Making disciples is not sexy, however. It is hard work, a daunting challenge in the best of conditions, and often difficult to measure. It's kind of like the difference between making babies and raising children. And I am well aware that in many cultural contexts sharing the good news can be quite dangerous. I'm simply trying to make the case that disciple-making and evangelism are two sides of the same coin. The Scriptures do not give us the freedom to choose between one or the other. It's both. Anything less is mission failure.

Here's another question: Is it the mission of the church to right social wrongs—after all, didn't Christ care for the poor and powerless? Absolutely. And unsurprisingly, when the church actually does the difficult work of genuine disciple making, we tend to see a lot of effort and resources directed toward addressing difficult social issues such as hunger, homelessness, and broken families from which flow so many terrible consequences.

Just look at the world to see who actually jumps into the most dreadful situations to offer hope. Think of all the victims devastated by sex trafficking, all of the abandoned children left to die on the side of a road or in a local dump. Think of all those who lose everything in a natural disaster. Christians do care and do respond, but they care and respond because they understand their responsibility as disciples of Christ.

Sadly, our efforts are often less than they should be. That is more often than not true, however, because we have done such a poor job of making disciples. Until we who identify as followers of Jesus Christ understand our stewardship responsibility, for example, or our responsibility to care for people in crisis (two things that are hard to miss when we actually study the Scriptures and determine to act on what we see), we will fail to act as we should. We fail, not so much because we don't care, but because we are not taught as disciples should be taught or called to act as disciples should act or held accountable for our actions as disciples should be.

I could add to my list, as could you. The key point here is simple. When the church fulfills her calling to make disciples, she will likely find herself acting more as the church should be acting.[1]

So, back to my "questions that should not be asked": *Why is the church so reluctant, or sadly, in many cases, so outright hostile to the kind of Christian schooling I have set out to describe in this book?* It doesn't make sense, especially given the unmistakable teaching of Scripture about how best to educate our children, the obviously imploding condition of our current culture, and the struggles of our churches to address the evident decline we see within and without.

I am puzzled and perplexed. I am not, however, clueless as to the forces at work both within and without the church. Since it is not the purpose of this book to address the culture "out there," I will leave that to others. It is the purpose of this book, however, to address the situation within the church. To do so I am going to respond to a number of oft-repeated reasons I hear from pastors and parents for rejecting the idea of Christian schooling. In doing so my goal will always be to "speak the truth in love" and to do so in as biblical a manner as possible.

Speaking the truth in love, however, does not mean that I will fail to speak with pointed clarity. Jesus always spoke the truth in love. On occasion, however, His language was strong enough to generate a powerfully negative response from those to whom He was speaking. He knew, however, that without truth people remain in disabling darkness. My goal, like His, is to shed light, not simply to generate conflict and disagreement.

## Where to Begin?

Part of what inspires me in this endeavor is the story of a man few know today but to whom all of us owe a debt of gratitude. His name: Ignaz Semmelwise. Semmelwise, a Hungarian physician who came to be called the "savior of mothers," discovered "that the incidence of puerperal fever, also known as childbed fever, could be drastically cut by the use of hand-washing standards in obstetrical clinics."[2]

As director of obstetrics at a hospital in Vienna, Semmelwise began to note that the incidence of puerperal fever was much lower in the section of his hospital where babies were delivered by midwives rather than by doctors. As he began to investigate the reasons behind this difference, he noted that doctors often came directly from dissecting patients who had died of infections to the ward where babies were being delivered. While an understanding of bacterial infection was still unknown, Semmelwise deduced that the doctors were somehow transferring something unhealthy to the mothers about to give birth.

In this day and age, we fully understand the ease with which bacteria and viruses can be transferred from one person to another. In the middle part of the 19th century, that was a complete unknown. What Semmelwise did see was a dramatic decline in the incidence of fever and a significantly lower death rate when the midwives and doctors under his direction began a rigorous hand-washing regimen.

Most of the young doctors under Semmelwise's leadership eagerly adopted his ideas. Unfortunately, most of the older doctors across Germany and Austria were not only resistant, but aggressively so. As a result, his ideas did not gain acceptance during his lifetime. Fortunately, within just a few decades, physicians and scientists like Joseph Lister, building on Semmelwise's research, were able to demonstrate the reality of bacteria and how the spread of bacteria through poor sanitation put many lives at risk.

Sadly, much like the resistance to Semmelwise's ideas, the reasons given by pastors, parents, and other critics for disregarding the idea of Christian schooling are many and varied. And like the opposition to Semmelwise's ideas, in the hands of particularly skilled opponents, especially those who occupy positions of influence, some of those arguments have proven powerful—so influential that the vast majority of Christian parents in the USA never even consider Christian schooling as an option for their children.

While I don't question the sincerity of those who make such arguments, I do question the foundation from which those arguments are made. I will not, therefore, hesitate to shed the light of Scripture, history, and culture on those assertions with the intent of demonstrating their flaws and weaknesses. I will do so because, like Ignaz Semmelwise, I simply cannot any longer ignore the carnage occurring all around me.

## A Framework for Moving Ahead

Before I begin to address the specific arguments I hear from parents and church leaders about why they do not personally embrace Christian schooling, I do want to reiterate two key thoughts. First of all, I want to do my best to allow the Scriptures to speak for themselves. For me this discussion is not about comparing notes or voicing opinions.

As Americans we are all entitled to our opinions. None of us, however, are entitled to our own facts. Either the Scriptures have something to say about the education and disciple making of our children or they don't.

If the Scriptures do speak to the why, what, and how of education and disciple-making, then as followers of Christ we do not have the right to simply ignore what we discover because it doesn't fit our personal or cultural norms and beliefs. Living according to the clear teaching of Scripture rather than the seductive norms of con-temporary culture is a problem in a whole host of areas. It is why the apostle Paul warns us that we must be constantly renewing our minds or we will find ourselves being crushed into the mold of the world (Romans 12:1–2).

A more troubling question, however, is this: What if, as many people claim, the Scriptures don't actually speak to this crucial issue? What if God, through His Son and in His Word, gave us a mission but didn't provide any real direction on how best to accomplish that mandate?

Now I wouldn't expect exact instructions. That wouldn't make sense given the vast differences between first-century Palestine or Rome and 21st-century America or Brazil or South Korea or Australia. While the details may be lacking, we should find the broad contours related to the why and the what and even some of the how. Other-wise, we are left to stumble ahead in utter darkness as to our Lord's intent. We become "the blind leading the blind," and we are thus condemned to "falling into the ditch."

Please permit me an obvious observation. God doesn't work that way. He speaks with clarity about even the most minor details of life. That is why the wisdom literature exists. It's why we have been given the didactic portions of the Scriptures. It's why the apostle Paul reminds his young disciple Timothy that all Scripture is given by inspiration of God and is profitable for all of life, not just for doctrinal discussions.[3]

To believe that our Lord would leave us without necessary direction for such a crucial aspect of life is to say that either He is incompetent at His job or has simply said, "Go thou and do whatever you want to do. It really doesn't matter to me." Neither of those options seems satisfactory.

A second key concept that should shape our thinking as we move ahead can be found in the oath we are asked to repeat when giving testimony in a court of law. It goes something like this: "I promise to tell the truth, the whole truth, and nothing but the truth." Ponder that pledge for just a moment.

Lots of people tell the truth but sometimes leave out important facts that would probably influence our thinking or decisions. Virtually all advertising and political posturing falls into that category. That statement can also encompass a lot of declarations that begin with the phrases "The research says" or "Experts say." As Mark Twain once remarked, "There are lies, damned lies, and statistics." A lot of what people claim for the research is simply not true. Nor are all experts really expert.

Equally problematic are the assertions that all of us make on occasion. Assertions are not arguments. To assert something does not make it so. I can't simply assert that education and discipleship are two sides of the same coin. I must instead prove that my assertion is reasonable, that it is backed by sound and thoughtful argument based on the best evidence available. That is my primary goal for this book.

## A List of Reasons

With that as a bit of an introduction, it is my goal in this next section to identify the common reasons I hear in discussions about Christian schooling. They are assertions raised against my premise that parents who identify as followers of Jesus Christ should ensure that their children receive an education that is thoroughly Christ-centered in focus, rigorous in nature, and which will adequately and appropriately prepare them for life, not just college or a career.

One final reminder as I move ahead in this book: I am not arguing that Christian parents should enroll their child in a Christian school. I can't make such an argument. Rather I am making the argument that Christian parents should ensure that their children receive a Christ-centered education. There are other means by which a parent can fulfill that obligation. I do believe, however, that Christian schools and homeschooling done well are by far the best options in our current cultural and historical context.

As I've said before, the people and activities that children and youth spend the most time with will shape their beliefs, values, and behavior. In that sense, whether we are aware of it or not, our children are already being discipled.

Here is a list of the most common reasons I hear from parents and church leaders. I will do my best to honestly express those assertions as fairly and honestly as I can and to respond to each assertion as graciously and biblically as I can. If in my efforts I offend any of my readers, and I suspect I may do so, I ask for your forgiveness. That is honestly not my intent.

- The Bible doesn't mandate Christian schools.
- We are called to be salt and light.
- Our kids need to experience the "real" world.
- I just don't see the difference.
- The quality and opportunities are just not as good.
- It costs too much money.
- Church and school are separate realms.
- My kids want to be with their friends.
- I attended a public school, and I turned out all right.
- My kids learn all they need to know about God from me and our pastors.
- As Christians we have a cultural responsibility to our local public schools.

So, let's plunge into these shark-infested waters.

## Reason #1: The Bible Doesn't Mandate Christian Schools.

The short response to this assertion is: of course not! With the exception of a few historical references, the Scriptures do not speak of schools as organizations. They do, however, speak extensively about schooling, as I've set out to demonstrate throughout this book.

This is an example of what I mean when I say that someone can tell the truth without telling the whole truth. Yes, it is true that there is no explicit command given in the Scripture to enroll a child in a Christian school. Such a command would make no sense given that few people in ancient times, unless they had significant wealth or position, could engage professional educators to teach their children. Schooling, such as it was, was largely a family affair or some kind of apprenticeship.

Such an assertion is also an example of how we sometimes allow our contemporary use of words such as education and discipleship to distort their true meaning. I will expand on that thought when I address the assertion that school and church are two different realms. So, while there is no "mandate" in Scripture requiring that children be enrolled in a Christian school, there are numerous mandates that they should receive a biblically infused, Christ-centered education.

## Reason #2: We are Called to Be Salt and Light.

Of all the assertions on my list, this is the one I hear most often and the one most often spoken with a sense of certainty and (forgive me) often with a sense of spiritual superiority. Who doesn't want their child or young person to be a light to the world? I certainly did, and do. I also understood, however, how difficult a task that is. I knew that they needed a high level of maturity, wisdom, insight, and courage—and training—if they were to fulfill that task well.

Permit me a few observations. First of all, I'm not sure that we really understand what Christ meant when He said, "You are the salt of the earth" and "You *are* the light of the world." Note the grammatical structure of those statements. Jesus doesn't say, "You need to be salt; you need to be light." Rather he says, "You are salt; you are light." The point He is making is actually pretty clear, though like so many other pretty-clear statements, we seem to often miss their true meaning.

Our kids don't "need" to *be* salt and light. They *are* salt and light. Just as their parents are salt and light. Just as pastors are salt and light. The idea here is that wherever we find ourselves, we are to be an honest reflection of the qualities and character of our Lord in such a way that we make a positive impact on those around us.

Followers of Christ can be that honest reflection anywhere they find themselves. Believe me when I say that there are lots of opportunities in every Christian school for students to bring savor and flavor to their context, just as there are many opportunities to provide light that brings glory to God. From personal experience I can tell you that there is no absence of personal pain and flawed thinking within the student body and the families of every Christian school in the US and around the world.

If that isn't enough of an opportunity for all the advocates of being salt and light, there are all kinds of community opportunities through athletics, the arts, and public service to give everyone a chance show the grace of God to a broken world. And those opportunities don't require being exposed in a systematic manner to grievous and life-killing error day after day.

Secondly, I think we need to consider with care what we do to our kids when we thrust them into a role for which they are not adequately prepared. To give you some perspective of what I mean, consider what virtually every legitimate evangelical mission-sending agency requires of its candidates before granting them approval to serve in a cross-cultural ministry. Now, consider that in spite of all that preparation and screening, the failure rate of first-term missionaries is nearly one in two. Yet we want to throw our kids into one of the most challenging cross-cultural contexts in the entire world, a secular public school, with little genuine preparation and virtually no meaningful support? It's crazy. In reality our kids are not missionaries so much as they are targets. And the current dropout rate in our churches lends credence to that reality.

Do some kids share their faith with their fellow students? Absolutely. Do some kids respond to the gospel as a result? Yes. There are two questions we need to ask, however: At what cost? And is there another way to accomplish the same outcomes? I think with a bit of creative thinking we could find a better way.

Thirdly, I think it's time to admit how hard it is for even adults to make an impact for Christ in America's secular school system, or anywhere else in the marketplace for that matter. The lunacy taking place in higher education, and it is lunacy, is making any kind of ministry effort increasingly difficult. It is not yet impossible for ministry organizations to function on college campuses, but the efforts to thwart those efforts have increased dramatically over the last ten years and show no signs of abating. And whatever happens in higher education eventually finds its way to our K–12 schools, indeed already has.

While not uniformly dark, our current state-funded, secular schools are still challenging places. They are, however, nearly as closed to the gospel as China and the former Soviet Union. It will take the same level of preparation, creativity, tenacity, and courage to take the light into those schools as has been true in taking the light of the gospel to those countries.

It is not, however, the work of novices. Until and unless our local churches are willing to do the hard work of genuinely preparing young people to step into that darkness and then providing ongoing and realistic support to those young people, we need to abandon the fiction that our kids on the whole are going to be effective missionaries in public schools.

Are there exceptions? Undoubtedly. Where there are those exceptions, however, it is because parents and churches have chosen to take on the monumental task of preparing and supporting those kids. And even in those situations, it is the rare kid who is able to survive, much less thrive. By the way, what evidence do we have about where those kids end up in the future? Much of value might be learned if we just did our homework.

## Reason #3: Our Kids Need to Experience the "Real" World.

I often hear this from the same people who want their kids to be salt and light. My first response, which I must sometimes suppress, is: "You've got to be kidding! You can't possibly believe that your local public school is, in any real sense, the 'real' world!" It's a fact that most college students discover in one way or another shortly after graduation. This reality reminds me of a *Frank and Ernest* cartoon I saw years ago. "School is mostly true and false questions, kid. Life is all essay questions."

School is like real life in much the same way that all of those Marvel comics made into movies are like real life or Disney movies are real life. There is a passing resemblance, but the rest is fantasy.

In this same vein, one of the objections hurled at Christian schools is that they are bubbles, hiding kids from the gritty reality of the "real" world. Francis Schaeffer had a good response to such foolishness. He once observed, "You can't build walls high enough to keep the world out." Unless you choose to go live on a desert island somewhere, it really is impossible to keep the "real" world from intruding into the world of your children.

Media of one form or another is a ubiquitous aspect of nearly every kid's life. Kids go shopping, attend sporting events and concerts, play with friends in the neighborhood or from church (some of whom have parents who don't fully share your values), go on vacation, visit family in other parts of the country, engage in public service or short-term mission projects, and play on local sports teams. Kids today see plenty of the "real" world without needing to be submerged in the grit and grime of contemporary secular schooling.

In reality, Christian schools are, or should be, "boot camps," places where kids are being prepared to step into that real world as mature, discerning adults. One of the interesting things about boot camp that applies equally to school is the careful preparation that precedes what are called "live-fire" drills. There are always training casualties as young men and women are preparing for military service. The purpose and structure of training, however, is to reduce the probability of those casualties. The same is true of the training and preparation that takes place in the context of genuine Christian schooling.

Permit me this question. Would we, as a country, ever consider sending untrained, poorly prepared, ill-equipped Scouts into battle against thoroughly trained, battle-hardened, well-equipped soldiers? If not, why would we send our kids into a battle for which they are not prepared? I can't think of a good answer to that question. Can you?

## Reason #4: I Just Don't See the Difference.

I often tell Christian school leaders and board members that in marketing efforts it is better to focus on outcomes than on inputs. Telling parents what will happen to their children during the school day is a good thing. Far better, however, is helping parents see the endgame—what kind of person their child will hopefully become as a result of what happens every day at school, especially when coupled with what happens at home and at their local church.

I'm the first to admit that far too many Christian schools have relied on an unhealthy form of legalism in the belief that information, rules, and structure alone can create the kind of transformational change we all hope to see in our kids. If that is all that we have in our arsenal, we are doomed to failure; and worse, we are certain to create a kind of inoculation that makes it difficult for true spiritual transformation to ever occur.

The question, however, is not so much how different Christian-schooled kids are from secular-schooled kids, but rather in which context is spiritual transformation most likely to happen. Now, I will freely admit that legalism, masquerading as spirituality, is as grievous a problem as secular education masquerading as truth. Both present a distorted picture of God, His purposes in this world, and our role in fulfilling those purposes. And both lead people into an abyss of one kind or another.

What we must take care in answering is this: In what kind of context is spiritual transformation more likely to occur? Is it in a place where Christ is banned and most people bring a flawed worldview to the conversation? Or is it in a place where Christ is exalted and most people bring a biblically sound worldview to the conversation?

Perhaps a simple agricultural illustration will suffice in answering that question. If you've ever planted a flower or vegetable garden, you know from experience that there are a couple of keys to success. First of all, you've got to plant in good soil, soil with the right kinds of nutrients and sufficient water. Bad soil = a bad harvest, no matter how hard you might work.

Secondly, you will need to continually and carefully do the work of cultivation if you hope to get the expected harvest. Such cultivation and care are not periodic endeavors. Constant attention is required. Such is the nature of life in a fallen world that we must always be on guard against the spiritual equivalent of weeds, insects, drought, hail, freezing temperatures—well, I think you get the idea.

Is every child and young person who is given a Christ-centered education spiritually healthier than every child who labors through a secular-centered education? Of course not. To make such a claim would be dishonest. I will, however, agree with the psalmist David when he wrote:

> Blessed is the man
> who walks not in the council of the wicked,
> nor stands in the way of sinners,
> nor sits in the seat of scoffers;
> but his delight is in the law of the LORD,
> and on his law he meditates day and night.
>
> He is like a tree
> planted by streams of water
> that yields its fruit in its season,
> and its leaf does not wither.
> In all he that he does, he prospers.
> The wicked are not so,
> but are like chaff that the wind drives away.
> (Psalm 1:1–4)

And remember, as the saying goes, "The proof of the pudding is in the eating." Aren't you glad that people don't judge you on the basis of your seventeen-year-old self? The purpose of Christian schooling is not to ensure the outcome. Rather, it is to plant the child in the right soil and nurture and cultivate with care on a daily basis for as long as we are given.

We're about halfway through my list of assertions. We'll address the remainder in the next chapter. Before I close this chapter, let me once again pose this question: As a parent, why wouldn't you want all the help you can get in equipping and preparing your children for life in this fallen world? Why turn your children over to "blind leaders of the blind" when you could immerse them in a world where Christ is exalted and truth is honestly explored? Why wouldn't you?

## For Reflection

1. What are the reasons you hear or give for not pursuing the Christian schooling of our children?

2. Why do you think it is so difficult to have a conversation around the topic of educating our children?

3. Do you believe it is beneficial to have our assumptions challenged? What's the best way of doing that?

4. If the mission of the church is to make disciples, how should that truth shape the various ministries you pursue at your church?

5. Please define and describe the "real" world. How best should we prepare our children for life in that world?

6. Would you want to be judged by your sixteen-year-old self? Why or why not?

7. Psalm 1 is such a key text. Read it carefully and consider what the text teaches us about what is necessary and what to avoid if we are to be established in a life of faith.

Chapter 9

## More Assertions, More Answers

As I write this chapter, we as a country have descended into a true national nightmare: the COVID-19 pandemic. In fact, I've heard and read dozens of typically thoughtful people declare this moment in history to be unprecedented. Those kinds of declarations cause alarm bells to go off inside my head. Unprecedented compared to what?

Compared to a great civil war that took the lives of over 600,000 soldiers and untold numbers of civilians, decimated large areas of our country, impoverished millions, and created animosities that still reverberate to this day?

Compared to two world wars that made those losses seem insignificant?

Or what of the 1918–19 flu pandemic that took the lives of an estimated 50–90 million people worldwide?

How about the millions of unborn children who have been sacrificed in the name of women's liberation since the infamous Roe v Wade decision of the Supreme Court?

So, how do we decide what is truly unprecedented, especially when so much of our modern secular world is drowning in misinformation promoted by people with personal agendas rather than a desire to get at what is true? That question, by the way, cuts both ways politically. Contrary to the view of many in the opinion business, neither progressives nor conservatives are exempt from shading the truth to make a partisan point.

Luke, the author of the New Testament book the Acts of the Apostles, gives us some insight into how best to answer that question in his narrative of the brief sojourn of Paul and Silas in the Macedonian community of Berea. In that account Luke notes the following: "The brothers [believers in Thessalonica] immediately sent Paul and Silas away by night to Berea, and when they arrived they went into the Jewish synagogue. Now these Jews were more noble than those in Thessalonica; they received the word with all eagerness, *examining the Scriptures daily to see if these things were so.*" [my emphasis] (Acts 17:10–11)

There are two key points I want to make about that text that apply to the theme of this book and especially apply to why I'm taking the time to respond to reasons people give for ignoring the importance of Christ-centered schooling for our children.

First, we need to note that the people in Berea, like most Jews in the Greco-Roman world, were well-acquainted with the Old Testament Scriptures. Unlike many in the current evangelical church who would have great difficulty identifying the twelve apostles or giving even a cursory chronological history of Christ's earthly ministry or making an argument for the resurrection of Christ, these people possessed the ability to take what Paul was teaching and compare it to what the Old Testament revealed of the coming Christ.

Second, because they were not only able, but willing, to exercise discernment in the pursuit of truth, Luke describes them as being "more noble" for that willingness. So, what made them "more noble"? It wasn't because they embraced Paul's teaching about Christ and the gospel. Nor was it because they rejected Paul's teaching on Christ. They were "more noble" because they put Paul's teaching to the test; they took what they heard and compared it to the proper measuring stick: the Old Testament.

As I pointed out in an earlier chapter, they had neither an open mind nor a closed mind. Rather they had a discerning mind, a mind that was shaped by the single standard of what was true. When they discovered that Paul's teaching aligned with what they knew to be true in the Old Testament, they then, and only then, embraced what he had to say.

John Stonestreet wrote, "Eighteenth-century British author Samuel Johnson called discernment 'the supreme end of education,' before offering the best definition I know of discernment: 'the power to tell the good from the bad, the genuine from the counterfeit, and to prefer the good and the genuine to the bad and the counterfeit.'"[1] That's a pretty good definition, one to which we should all aspire.

I do not claim to be writing under the inspiration of the Holy Spirit in the same way that Paul wrote and spoke. I am, however, trying to get people to step back from their preconceived notions—ideas often based on a flawed and incomplete understanding of what the Scriptures have to say about Christian schooling. Only when we do that, only when we carefully compare those beliefs with the teaching of Scripture rather than with the assertions of modern culture, can we, like the Bereans, be considered "noble."

Thus, in this chapter, I will continue to address the assertions I hear from parents, pastors, and other Christian leaders about the idea of formal Christian schooling versus a monumentally biased secular education. I do so with the hope that some of what I have to say will give people pause before simply dismissing the entire enterprise.

## Reason #5: The Quality and Opportunities Are Just Not Good Enough.

Several years ago, I was speaking at a church on the topic of Christian schooling. At the conclusion of my message, I was approached by a father who, with tears in his eyes, shared an all-too-familiar story with me. For years his son had attended the Christian school sponsored by the church he attended. After his freshman year in high school, however, the family had reached a mutual agreement that the quality of education offered by that school was just not very good. In addition, there were courses that their son needed in preparation for his college major that the school did not offer.

Nearly three years later, that son was about to graduate from the local public high school with honors and had been accepted at the college of his choice—all good things, of course. The father then posed this question to me: Did we make the right choice? Here's how I responded: "That is a tough decision that no Christian family should have to make. No child or young person should have to sacrifice a quality education in pursuit of a supposedly Christ-centered education. As a parent you must make decisions in the light of Scripture that you see as best for your child. That is clearly what you did."

Of all the reasons parents give for not enrolling their child in a Christian school, this is the one that most breaks my heart. In some cases, as with one of my grand-daughters, many Christian schools do not offer the kind of specialized instruction required to meet the legitimate learning needs of some students. And most families certainly can't provide that instruction in a homeschool context. Thus, a parent is left with no real option but to enroll the child in a local public school. Sadly, however, the special-needs programs offered in the public system can, and do, vary widely in terms of quality and impact.

Beyond those special-needs kids, far too many Christian schools simply do not deliver a quality education of even the basics. By quality I do not mean that they don't offer an equivalent variety of course offerings as a local public school. In my opinion, too much emphasis is being placed on the idea that "more is better." What I do believe essential is an excellent, enriching teaching-learning environment in which students are encouraged to grow personally and spiritually, challenged to think deeply, prodded to ask insightful questions, and inspired to produce quality work.

That vision of a good education requires exceptional teachers, teachers who understand that they can't simply show up and do what they have done for the last decade. They are teachers who recognize that they need to be constantly refining their skills, deepening their knowledge, and creating an engaging environment. They are teachers who do not insist on conformity but who encourage discernment in pursuit of wisdom, understanding, and knowledge.

Any vision of a good education also takes into account necessary resources. I'm not much impressed with educational bling, but I do believe that there are certain resources that are essential to providing a quality education at this time in history. I do think we have become overdependent on technology, but to ignore the impact of technology on every aspect of life is unwise at best.

Two concluding remarks. As someone has observed, "God don't make no junk"— not very eloquent, but very much on target. I strongly declare that Christian schools that fail to uphold the highest standards of education are by definition not Christian. Using a lack of resources as an excuse for failing to provide a quality education is simply unacceptable. Those schools present a distorted view of the very Lord they say they revere and thus do great harm to the very students they say they want to serve.

On the other side of the conversation, far too many parents have been seduced by educational bling and have come to believe that their child simply won't make it in the world without all the bells and whistles that might be provided at the local public school. As one observer put it, "In the end, the legions of education critics who incessantly pester the schools to make dramatic changes would do well to remember one central fact: At its core, education is a people process. Yes, youngsters need tools, but most of all they need people."[2]

Give me great teachers with a heart for God any day over the most well-equipped biology or chemistry lab. The best education is achieved in a life-on-life context. Great teachers always find a way to inspire their students to pursue excellence while giving them the tools necessary to accomplish that important goal. And that is what happens in a truly Christ-centered educational environment.

This conversation, however, inevitably brings us to the next assertion on my list.

## Reason #6: It Just Costs Too Much.

Exceptional quality always comes with a price tag, and that price tag doesn't just equal money spent. It can also include time spent. Great teachers, for example, spend a lot of time in preparation for instruction and even more time in coaching and encouraging students to success.

As with any classroom teacher, parents who choose the homeschooling option must understand the enormous investment of time, energy, and creativity necessary to successfully fulfill their obligation. There are simply no shortcuts to excellence. There is always a price to pay. And because of the way we, in the USA, have chosen to fund the education of our children, parents who would even consider choosing Christian schooling for their children are the ones who must pay that price—whether with their checkbook, with their time, or more realistically with both. Sadly, but in many cases understandably, that is a price far too few evangelical parents are willing, or in many cases able, to pay.

That is understandable because schooling of any kind is costly, and there are many parents who would choose Christian schooling for their children but simply can't afford to do so. Now I want to make a careful distinction at this point: There is a big difference between people who can't afford Christian schooling because they have chosen to pursue other priorities like new and expensive cars, homes beyond their means, exotic vacations, or any number of other of life's pleasures, and people who are genuinely challenged financially.

In his book *The Benedict Option*, Rod Dreher makes a telling observation. "If you want to know how critical education is to cultural and religious survival, ask the Jews. Rabbi Mark Gottlieb says, 'Jews committed to traditional life put schooling above almost anything. There are families that will do just about anything short of bankrupting themselves to give their children an Orthodox Jewish education.' Christians have not been nearly as alert to the importance of education, and it's time to change that."[3]

For some parents, however, pursuit of Christian schooling for their children is truly beyond their financial means. That is especially, though not exclusively, true of many families in urban settings. I am personally familiar with this challenge. As a high school student at Dade Christian School in Miami, Florida, in the mid-1960s, I was only able to attend because the church and school provided me with a part-time janitorial job after school and on Saturdays. I only made a dollar an hour, but it was enough to pay for a portion of my tuition. Without that job, I would not have been able to attend, and that was at a time when the price tag for a year's tuition was less than $1,000 a year.

The challenge, of course, is that schooling is just not affordable, at least as long as we choose to have teachers in the classroom. Education is a people-intensive endeavor. Something like 70–80% of every school's budget (public or private) is the cost of labor. And believe me, as one who spent many years in the classroom, teachers are not compensated well, especially in Christian schools. Thus, if we want to decrease costs, we must be willing to decrease the human element in education. I for one don't believe that to be wise.

There is, of course, more adding to the price tag associated with traditional education. There are buildings that require ongoing maintenance, upkeep, insurance, and utility costs. There is the ever-increasing cost of curriculum and instruction, including the price of staying current with technology. Adding to the upward pressure on costs are all of the programs including athletics, the fine arts, and special-education programs that everyone sees as crucial to providing a well-rounded education.

As a result, parents are asking the question, is it worth it? And more and more, the answer is coming back a resounding No! If, however, as I am arguing in this book, it's not only worth it but is necessary, then we simply can't throw up our hands and walk away.

Adding to the problem, at least in my opinion, has been the reluctance, and in some cases the active resistance, of the "church" when it comes to discussions related to Christian schooling, especially to the idea of Christian schools. Indeed, that reluctance and resistance has been a major motivation behind the writing of this book, which leads me to consider the next reason on my list.

## Reason #7: Church and School Are Separate Realms and Should Remain So.

What so astonishes me is a simple historical fact. At no other time and in no other place has the "church" so separated education and discipleship as has been true in the USA since at least the 1840s. That is a topic I will address in the next chapter. The consequences that flow from that "divorce" are, however, real, and impact the ability of Christian schools to make education more accessible to more people.

Permit me to pose a question that haunted me during a time of deep study in the book of Acts. Have you ever wondered why God chose Saul of Tarsus to serve as the "apostle to the Gentiles"? Why not Peter? Why not John? Why not any of the other apostles? The Scriptures do not provide us an explicit answer. It is, however, a question on which a bit of speculation might prove worthwhile.

Contrary to the image many people have that the apostles were a group of under-educated men, they were, as were most Jewish men, like those in Berea, well-educated in terms of what today's scholars call biblical theology, much more so than the average man or woman in the average evangelical church in the USA today. What John and Peter lacked that Saul of Tarsus possessed, however, was what we today would call a liberal arts education.

Tarsus was a university town, much like Boston or Chicago or New York. It was home to one of the finest schools of higher education in the Greco-Roman world, and Saul was likely a graduate. His knowledge of literature, understanding of philosophy, and grasp of culture are apparent in virtually all of his letters to the churches and thus give testimony to that reality.

In reading those letters, you get no sense that Paul sets one aspect of knowledge (theology) apart from another aspect of knowledge (philosophy or literature). Thus, he encourages the followers of Christ to "destroy arguments and every lofty opinion raised against the knowledge of God, and take every thought captive to obey Christ . . ." [4]

In his letter to the church in Colossae, Paul issues this warning: "See to it that no one takes you captive by philosophy and empty deceit, according to human tradition, according to the elemental spirits of the world and not according to Christ." [5] He does so because the "elemental spirits of the world" can be so seductive. Again, it's why we are warned against being "conformed to this world" but encouraged to "be transformed by the renewing of [our] mind" so that we "may discern what is the will of God, what is good and acceptable and perfect." [6]

In those passages Paul is not in any way limiting our thinking to theological topics. Rather, he has a much broader view in mind. Since Christ is Lord of all, not just some truncated vision of a particular aspect of the world, we must understand the world, as Christ understands the world, in its totality. We must do this so that we can discern the will of God in all areas of life. And we do that so we can know what is good and acceptable and perfect to the heart and mind and will of our Lord. To do anything less is to diminish the Lordship of Christ in this present age.

That, by the way, is exactly what the secular power structures in the USA and the rest of the world want us to do. They want us to stay hidden away in our private little enclaves, singing our praise songs, and greeting one another with a smile and pious words. They most assuredly do not want us shining the light of God's Word on the darkness of a world broken by sin. We are told it's OK to do good deeds when a crisis strikes; just don't speak publicly into the moral and intellectual rot of the day.

Sadly, we not only acquiesce to that demand, but with the exception of a few brave and intellectually prepared individuals, we don't really seem to have much to say. We embrace the gospel, as we should, but we tend to ignore the wisdom literature of both the Old and the New Testaments. Down our current path lie irrelevance and diminishing impact for Christ in the world.

This is obviously a much larger topic than is possible to explore in this context. It is a topic, however, that we can no longer afford to ignore. The consequences are just too severe. We can no longer accept the facile idea that on one side we have "spiritual" truth and on the other side we have "secular" knowledge. There is no bright line between the two—nor should there be a bright line in how we educate our children. To continue on our current path is to put our children and young people at great risk and to fail at our calling to make disciples.

## Reason #8: My Kids Want to Be With Their Friends.

If there is one false and flawed secular idea that has taken deep root in the hearts and minds of evangelical parents, it is this: Kids know best. A second equally bad idea is this: Kids need to be happy. Combined, these ideas have led parents to make many poor decisions regarding their children.

In reality, the Scriptures remind us that "Foolishness is bound up in the heart of a child but the rod of correction will drive it far from him."[7] I know that this particular passage has been misread, leading many parents to use inappropriate approaches to discipline. The fundamental truth of the text cannot, however, be ignored: Children are born into sin and are, therefore, prone, as the hymnwriter reminds us, "to wander."

Our job as parents is, therefore, to ensure that our children are equipped to think and live wisely in light of the Scriptures. It is not to give in to their whims or desires. Rather, it is to help shape their thinking about what is most important in the world. Friends are important. Indeed, they are so important that Proverbs remind us to choose friends carefully and to value friendships with people who will always tell us the truth and encourage us to be our best in every area of life.

Helping our children to make wise choices regarding friends is one of the greatest responsibilities we bear as parents. We need to help them see the qualities that make for true friends as well as help them recognize the qualities that they should avoid when choosing friends. And when responding to the statement, "You don't have the right to choose who I can be friends with," as parents we need to have the courage to say firmly but graciously, "Yes, yes we do."

In reality, when we do set out to help our children understand the value and nature of true friendship, we are likely to find that our children do make good friendship choices. To make decisions about the education of our children based on their demand to "be with my friends" is, however, to surrender our God-given stewardship responsibility to "bring up a child in the discipline and instruction of the Lord."[8]

Making wise choices about friends is never easy, even for mature adults. One constant to consider, however, is the impact the wrong kind of companion can make on anyone's life. Consider the following thoughts from Proverbs:

- He who walks with wise men will be wise, but the companions of fools will suffer harm. (Proverbs 13:20)
- Leave the presence of a fool, or you will not discern words of knowledge. The wisdom of the prudent is to understand his ways, but folly of fools is deceit. Fools mock at sin, but among the upright there is good will. (Proverbs 14:7–9)
- A man of many friends comes to ruin, but there is a friend who sticks closer than a brother. (Proverbs 18:24)
- Faithful are the wounds of a friend, but deceitful are the kisses of an enemy. (Proverbs 27:6)

It isn't complicated. The people we choose to hang around, that our children choose to hang around, can and often do have a huge impact on the choices we make in our lives. So, choose carefully. Choose people of wisdom, discernment, and grace. Avoid the fool, the angry, the arrogant. In a very real sense, your life and the life of your child will depend on those choices.

## Reason #9: I Attended a Secular Public School, and I Turned Out OK.

Here I step onto a field in which are buried numerous landmines. It's a bit like responding to the proverbial question, "Have you stopped beating your wife?" There is no good answer.

Permit me, however, to go ahead and step onto that dangerous terrain. I could respond by saying, "Yes, you appear to be little damaged by your experience." Or I could respond and say, "Well, that is a matter of opinion." In either case, however, I would have missed the main point. Lots of people survive, even thrive, after experiencing difficult, even terrible situations and circumstances. God's grace is, after all, the most transformative power in the entire world. Returning to an early thought, however, I am utterly taken by our Lord's words about the terrible price of causing little ones to stumble.[9]

Like it or not, the more you allow your children to be exposed to error, the greater the likelihood that they will at some point stumble, or that they will follow a spiritually blind teacher into the ditch.[10] Regardless of our personal experiences, we do not have the freedom to do as we choose with our children. We must, as good stewards of God's gracious gift, fulfill our responsibility to our Lord, and that requires us to ensure that our children are systematically exposed to what is true and good and beautiful, as defined by God's Word, not as defined by the outcomes of some state-sponsored secular curriculum.

Let me take a further step onto that dangerous turf. I find that a lot of good and godly people, people who are to some extent doctrinally sound, are nonetheless fairly secular in their general view of the world and their place in the world. That observation would include a lot of pastors.

I'm actually stunned at the number of people who have little or no idea of how the Scriptures should shape how we see the world of work and commerce in which we are immersed on a daily basis. Or how the Scriptures should shape how we view the role of government in our lives. Or the arts. Or the idea of truth in general. Or any of the other arenas in which we dwell on a daily basis.

If Jesus is Lord over all things, doesn't it make sense that we should develop an awareness for how He views "all things"? While the Scriptures aren't exhaustive in explaining everything about everything under the sun, they do give us insights that should lead to wisdom and discernment about all things. No, the Bible is not a biology textbook or an economics textbook, but there are insights from the nature of God and His role in creation that should inform all of us about God's role in both biology and economics.

Yes, the main theme of Scripture is the scope of God's redemptive work in the world. That is not, however, all that God has for us in His Word. Without careful instruction, which many attending our churches today have not received, we will miss so much of God's mind about our role in the world and in advancing His purposes in the world. Christian schooling done right allows us to connect the secular and the sacred in a way that a periodic sermon can't.

## Reason #10: My Kids Learn What They Need to Know About God From Us and the Pastors at Our Church.

I enjoy playing golf. Like a recent commercial says, "I'm only OK," but I enjoy the game. I'm of the age that my first introduction to the game came at a time when Arnold Palmer was the most prominent and successful professional golfer in the USA. In fact, my first set of clubs was a set of Wilson Arnold Palmer Signature clubs. Sadly, they didn't come with Arnold's gift for the game.

To better learn to use those clubs and the other more forgiving clubs I now possess, I needed to get some instruction from someone who knew a bit about the game. I did more than that, however. I began to subscribe to several golf magazines, in which I could read articles about the game and how best to play the game. I must also confess that I watch golf tournaments on television. I don't do so just to be entertained, but because in watching those who actually play the game well, I learn a lot. In other words, I have chosen to immerse myself in the world of golf.

You may question whether that is a good or poor use of my time. You might be right to ask that question. I would suspect, however, that anyone reading this book who enjoys a particular activity or hobby has done much the same thing. If you want to get good at something, you immerse yourself in that activity and seek to learn from as many people as possible about how to get better at what you are trying to do. Why would we want anything less for our children when it comes to their walk of faith?

That insight is, by the way, why an ever-increasing number of parents are opting for what we call homeschooling. They want to immerse their children in their world, a world defined and shaped by their values that are, hopefully, in turn shaped by the Word of God. I have great admiration for parents willing to take on the task of educating their children. I do wish more of those parents fully understood the challenges inherent in the task they have chosen to undertake because I'm not always sure that they do.

Why would I say that? I do so because I'm not sure that parents always grasp a full understanding of the concept of immersion. I've shared the data on how much time our children spend with us as parents and at church compared with the time they spend with media, friends, and school. There is no comparison. As a result, the world in which these kids are immersed usually has little to do with their parents and even less with their church.

In the agrarian, small-community world in which most people dwelt for most of human history, most kids, for good or ill, were immersed in their parents' world. Only the very rich would have lived in a home where children had their own bedroom into which they could retreat and isolate themselves from parents or siblings. Indeed, as recently as the 1950s, the size of the average single-family home was a pretty meager 900 square feet, contained a single bathroom, a single phone that was located in a very public place, and maybe a single television set on which everyone watched the same shows. Given that reality, it was hard to escape immersion in your parents' world.

Go just a blink back in time historically from that 1950s home, and most parents worked out of their own home, either in an agricultural setting or a small shop. Parents didn't commute to work until the advent of the Industrial Revolution. I don't want to oversimplify or romanticize that historic reality, but let's be honest about our current reality. Parents simply have less time to spend with their kids today than was true in the slower pace of the agrarian, small-town world that characterized much of human history.

That doesn't mean that parents took advantage of that reality. Indeed, many didn't. But the opportunity for greater engagement with children and young people was possible in ways that aren't as likely today given the impact of industrialization and technology. Parents still have the possibility of significant impact on their kids. I think it only wise, however, to pay attention to what one dad said to me while trying to think of how best to describe the purpose of the school where he sent his kids: "We can't do it alone."

He is right. You can't do it alone. God doesn't intend you to do so. And why would you want to? Why not take advantage of the power of a godly community in helping you "bring up your children in the discipline and instruction of the Lord"? I can think of no good reason for refusing that help.

## Reason #11: As Christians, We Have a Cultural Obligation to Support Public Education.

Many years ago, I worked with a Christian school in a small town in Texas. My dad's family is from the Hill Country in central Texas, from Bandera County specifically, so I am quite familiar with what that looks like. While working with that school, I had the opportunity to interview the pastor of a large Baptist church in that town. It was during that conversation that I heard a passionate presentation of this argument.

In fact, during that conversation this pastor went so far as to tell me that most people in his church referred to the school with which I was working as the "cult on the hill." Now remember, this school was not run by the local Jehovah's Witnesses, Christian Scientists, or a nearby Mormon church. No, this school was operated by a thoroughly evangelical group committed to the goal of helping students develop a sound biblical worldview.

Their single crime, apparently, was that they chose not to be part of the local public system, where the vast majority of the children from the local evangelical churches attended. It reminded me a bit of how earlier generations of evangelical pastors spoke of local Catholic schools—many of which had specific ethnic foundations—as something less than fully American. It was a sad thing then, and is no less so today.

I do believe that local churches should find ways to minister to local public schools, especially urban schools. They are, after all, among the neediest of mission fields in our country. I will address this idea more fully in my final chapter. For now, let me say that such an approach can be a powerful tool in spreading the gospel.

In fact, it was a tool God used to spread the gospel in the face of considerable persecution during the first, second, and third centuries. During those times of plagues, the pagan priests would, as we would say today, head for the hills. They were unwilling to put their lives at risk for the people they were supposed to serve. In contrast, those who were followers of Christ stepped into the danger and saved many lives, even when so doing cost many of those early Christians their own lives.

As Rodney Stark observes in his book *The Triumph of Christianity*, "the classical philosophers had nothing useful to say except to blame it all on fate. . . . But Christians claimed to have answers and, most of all, they took appropriate action . . . [they] met the obligation to care for the sick rather than desert them, and thereby saved enormous numbers of lives!" And as he goes on to note, "This surely must have produced some conversions, especially among those who were nursed back to health."[11]

So, to pastors I would say, "Be bold, seek every opportunity for the adults and even mature young people in your church to step in and provide genuine help to kids in genuine need. It does make a difference. Doing something like that doesn't, however, require that you sacrifice your children and young people to the 'culture god.'" Remember, both pastors and parents are given an incredibly important responsibility. You are both stewards and shepherds. Turning your children over to a thoroughly secular system for their education fails at both tasks. You can do better—indeed must do better.

## How Did We Get Here?

One of the things that strikes me so powerfully when I engage in conversations with pastors and parents is the complete lack of understanding of the historical context from which the current structure of schooling in the USA was forged. In the next chapter I am going to try to bring some clarity to the question, How did we get here?

## For Reflection

1. If, as Samuel Johnson, asserts, "the supreme end of education" is to have discernment, is it possible to truly achieve that end apart from God's Word?

2. Why do you think that education is so expensive? What goes into the cost of your child's education? Which of those things are necessary in your opinion? Which are not? Defend your answers from the Scriptures.

3. Are the church and the school two separate realms? Or might they be two sides of the same coin in pursuit of a common objective: making disciples? Think carefully and biblically rather than relying on personal and cultural assumptions to answer that question.

4. Given current reality, do you believe as a parent or as a pastor that you can truly and effectively fulfill your disciple-making responsibilities alone?

Chapter 10

# How Did We Get Here?

Where is Daniel Webster when we need him? If that name is unfamiliar to you, then you probably attended a state-funded public school in the 1980s or later. Of course, most of you (I hope) would recognize the name Webster attached to the famous dictionary, though it was Noah, not Daniel, who created that well-known resource. My question relates more to one of the most famous fictional trials in American history: Jabez Stone v Mr. Scratch, aka the devil.

Stephen Vincent Benet, in his celebrated work *The Devil and Daniel Webster*, tells the tale of a poor New England Farmer, Jabez Stone, who after many dismal years decides to make a pact with the devil, who appears in the form of a Mr. Scratch. The details of the agreement are simple. In return for seven years of prosperity, Farmer Stone agrees to sell his soul.

In the story as told by Benet, the devil is true to his word. Indeed, for seven years Jabez Stone experiences incredible prosperity, which he generously shares with many of his neighbors. On the day appointed, however, Mr. Scratch returns to conclude the bargain and drag Farmer Stone off to his "just" reward.

As anyone would expect, farmer Stone is not eager to experience the consequences of his tragic and shortsighted agreement. Mr. Scratch, however, producing the signed agreement, insists, as is his right, that Stone pay up on the agreement. It is at this point that Stone convinces Daniel Webster, a well-known attorney, to argue his case in an unusual court of law. Webster agrees, argues eloquently and persuasively before a rather interesting judge and jury, and eventually wins acquittal for Farmer Stone.

*The Devil and Daniel Webster* is, of course, a work of fiction, one we might read with a sense of amusement. Sadly, however, the idea of making a bargain with the devil is not always a fiction. Sometimes it is a reality. And sometimes the consequences are real. Let me tell you of one such bargain. One that is not fictional in nature. One that has come with high costs.

## The Way It Was

For most of two centuries from the time the Pilgrims and Puritans began to arrive in the New World, education was a truly local affair. For much of that time, formal schooling took place in the home, similar to the homeschooling of our day, or in the study of a local pastor. There were few schools as we today would understand schools. Even the famous one-room schoolhouse had not yet made its appearance. In the early decades of the 19th century, that began to change.

The desire to build a unified system of public schools was actually quite strong among the early framers of the new American society. Dr. Benjamin Rush, a signatory of the Declaration of Independence and member of the Pennsylvania delegation to the Constitutional Convention, arguing in favor of such a system, observed, "We have changed our forms of government, but it remains yet to effect a revolution in our principles, opinions, and manners to accommodate them to the forms of government we have adopted."[1] Thus the goal of producing citizens for the new republic became a motivation for the establishment of a unified system of public schools. As we will see, however, there was a very specific definition of what those citizens would look like, what they would believe, and how they would act.

There was, however, significant resistance to such a system. Quite simply, that resistance crystalized around the reality that early 19th-century America, as is true today, was divided by dozens of religious and ethnic groups, all espousing a variety of competing interpretations of the Bible, and was further divided by an increasing number of people who chose no faith at all. As a consequence, not everyone was interested in some kind of one-size-fits-all school system.

Thomas Jefferson, certainly one of our key and influential founding fathers, proposed a solution to that problem: Eliminate those differences through education. As McCarthy, Skillen, and Harper observed in their book *Disestablishment a Second Time: Genuine Pluralism for American Schools*, "The clear implication is that Jefferson's religion [a form of deism embraced by many of the country's political and intellectual leaders in the early 19th century] could become universal [but] only if other claims to 'true religion' were gradually dropped. Short of that, however, Jefferson's religion could function as the universal common denominator, in authority realm if *all other religious groups admitted to its authority while remaining satisfied to hold on to their own peculiar dogmas in a limited, private, non-universal realm*"[2] [my emphasis].

Put simply, Jefferson was intent on creating a system of publicly funded education with the goal of promoting and promulgating a particular view of the world, a view that was consistent with his own, a view that elevated human reason above any other way of knowing. Consider the following statements from Mr. Jefferson:

- I have so much confidence in the good sense of man, and his qualifications for self-government, that I am never afraid of the issue where reason is left free to exert her force. (*letter to Comte Diodati*, 1789)
- No experiment can be more interesting than that we are now trying, and which we trust will end in establishing the fact, that man may be governed by reason and truth. (*letter to John Tyler*, 1804)
- God has bestowed reason . . . as the umpire of truth. (*letter to Miles King*, 1814)
- Our opinions are not voluntary. Every man's own reason must be his oracle. (*letter to Benjamin Rush*, 1813)
- Every man's reason is his own rightful umpire. This principle, with that of acquiescence in the will of the majority, will preserve us free and prosperous as long as they are sacredly observed. (*letter to John F. Watson*, 1814)
- Everyone must act according to the dictates of his own reason. (*letter to Samuel Miller*, 1808)
- Man once surrendering his reason, has no remaining guard against absurdities the most monstrous, and like a ship without a rudder, is the sport of every wind. With such a person, gullibility, which they call faith, takes the helm from the hand of reason, and the mind becomes a wreck. (*letter to James Smith*, 1822)

I would ask you to contrast that last quote with a similar idea from the pen of the apostle Paul, who writes,

> And he gave the apostles, the prophets, the evangelists, the shepherds and teachers to equip the saints for the work of ministry, for building up the body of Christ, until we all attain to the unity of the faith and the knowledge of the Son of God, to mature manhood, to the measure of the fullness of Christ, so that we may no longer be children carried about by every wind of doctrine, by human cunning, by craftiness in deceitful schemes. Rather, speaking the truth in love, we are to grow up in every way into him who is the head, into Christ. (Ephesians 4:11–15)

I suspect that most people can see the clear contradiction between the argument for reason as the primary arbiter for deciding what is good and beautiful and true as espoused by Jefferson and viewing those same ideas through revelation, through the lens of Scripture, to determine what is good and beautiful and true.

I don't write this as a criticism of Jefferson's, and later Horace Mann's, desire for ensuring that all children receive a quality education. I heartily agree with that desire. As Jefferson also observed, "I think it is Montaigne who has said, that ignorance is the softest pillow on which a man can rest his head" (*letter to Edmund Randolph*, 1794). He was wise to say that, "If a nation expects to be ignorant and free in a state of civilization, it expects what never was and never will be" (*letter to Charles Yancey*, 1816).

The issue that I raise is not whether all children should receive a sound, thorough education. Rather what concerns me in this book is upon what foundation that sound, thorough education will be built. For Jefferson, and later Mann, the foundation was human reason. For those who would follow Christ, that foundation is more than human reason alone. Life is also to be built on the revelation of God found in the Scriptures, both the Old and the New Testaments, in Jesus Christ, the Word made flesh, and then finally in creation itself, as the apostle Paul instructs us when he writes,

> For the wrath of God is revealed from heaven against all ungodliness and unrighteousness of men, who by their unrighteousness suppress the truth. For what can be known about God is plain to them, because God has shown it to them. For his invisible attributes, namely his eternal power and divine nature, have been clearly perceived, ever since the creation of the world, in the things that have been made. So they are without excuse. For although they knew God, they did not honor him as God or give thanks to him, but they became futile in their thinking, and their foolish hearts were darkened. Claiming to be wise they became fools, and exchanged the glory of the immortal God for images resembling mortal man and birds and animals and creeping things. (Romans 1:18–23)

That is the end to which reason untethered from true truth always leads. It is the end to which our current system of public education will inevitably lead, indeed is leading. The reason why that is true is not terribly difficult to grasp once we more fully look beneath the surface of Jefferson's language. Francis Schaeffer helps us do that: "Schaeffer defined rationalism as 'the system whereby men and women, beginning absolutely by themselves, try rationally to build out from themselves, having only Man as their integration point, to find all knowledge, meaning and value."[3]

Please don't get lost in that sentence. Its meaning, with but a moment of reflection, becomes clear. If man becomes the means by which we measure all things, we are doomed to view the world as through a fractured mirror because all people are, as a result of the fall, broken.

I love how Eugene Petersen describes this reality: "Long before we ever got around to asking questions about God, God has been questioning us. Long before we got interested in the subject of God, God subjected us to the most intensive and searching knowledge. Before it ever crossed our minds that God might be important, God singled us out as important. Before we were formed in the womb, God knew us. We are known before we know."

He goes on with this key insight: "This realization has a practical result: no longer do we run here and there, panicked and anxious, searching for the answers to life. Our lives are not puzzles to be figured out. Rather, we come to God, who knows us and reveals to us the truth of our lives. The fundamental mistake is to begin with ourselves and not God. God is the center from which all of life develops. If we use our ego as the center from which to plot the geometry of our lives, we will live eccentrically."[4]

The implications for how we educate our children from both Schaeffer and Petersen are profound. I could take you through a detailed history of how our philosophical approach to education has continued to evolve since Jefferson and Mann through John Dewey and his disciples, who today largely populate our colleges of education. If you desire to engage in such a study, there are a number of books I would suggest for you to read and study.[5]

My goal for this book is, however, much more focused. From the beginning I have argued that the purpose for schooling as revealed in the Scriptures is nearly 180 degree opposite from the current framework that drives how we educate our children in America's public schools. The consequences of those differences have finally reached a place where it is becoming increasingly difficult to ignore—though many parents and pastors continue to keep their heads, like the infamous ostrich, planted firmly in the sand. It is much easier to blame the "media" or the "academy" (referring to higher education) than to acknowledge the clear connection between the progressive approach to schooling that predominates in our K–12 public system and what we see in the culture around us.

This willful blindness was highlighted in a recent editorial in *World* magazine. The title of that article—"A Socialist Future? If America Has One, Our K–12 Public Schools Will Be One of the Big Factors"—is absolutely right on target. In that editorial, Joel Belz asks a probing question about how we have reached a place where over fifty percent of our young people see the free market system as bad and socialism as good. He writes, "So, are we being called to believe that some gigantic conspiracy is at work?"

His answer to his own question is truly insightful. "Hardly. This is a worldview, so far-reaching, so unwieldy, with so many nuances, that no world leader could conceivably coordinate all its facets, over such relatively long time periods and geographic distances. The movement has operated—mostly in the open—longer than most of us have been around. When you dominate the landscape as it has, you don't need to operate in the dark. Sometimes, when you're that big, folks just think you're part of the natural order of things."[6]

To what movement is he referring? It is the American public school system. And we are foolish to ignore that reality because, as Belz notes, "when you total up the impact exerted on a young girl or boy over 180 days a year, for 13 years, you can almost ignore the need to gather, analyze, and evaluate the content of that instruction. Just think about the colleges and universities that shaped most of the educators in today's schools, and you understand why so many educators sound like socialists. Their students are profoundly shaped not just by the content of the classes, but maybe even more so by their day-to-day intergenerational contact. Students learn by that whole experience that yes, it's government's duty to do this thing called 'education.' Nobody needs to call it 'socialism'; we learn that along the way while we watch it happening."[7]

I once again call you to consider a simple reality: "Can a blind man lead a blind man? Will they not both fall into a pit? A disciple is not above his teacher, but everyone when he is fully trained will be like his teacher" (Luke 6:39–40). That is what Belz is saying in his article and what I've been trying to say throughout this book.

This is a serious problem that we have ignored for too long. It is long past time for Christ-followers to at least begin to ask questions about what has been happening in and through our public-school system for several generations now. To that end I want to make two observations before moving on to that "pact with the devil" the evangelical church made in the 1840s that opened the door to our current challenges.

First of all, as stated earlier, Christian schooling is not shielding our children from the realities of life; rather it is about inculcating in them an understanding of how we can know what is good and beautiful and true, of how we can distinguish truth from error, and then live life according to that reality. Remember my mantra: Christian schooling is not a bubble; it is intended to be a boot camp. Rather than focusing on that flawed belief about the purpose of Christian schooling, it is time for us to grasp the key reality that what is at stake in our present situation is the very concept of truth.

In fact, it has been argued that, "The present chasm between generations has been brought about almost entirely by a change in the concept of truth. . . The consensus about us is almost monolithic, whether you review the arts, literature or simply read the newspapers and magazines [and in today's world the internet]. On every side you can feel the stranglehold of this new methodology—and by 'methodology' we mean the way we approach truth and knowing. The tragedy of our situation today is that men and women [and I would add most powerfully our children and young people] are being fundamentally affected by the new way of looking at truth, and yet they have never even analyzed the drift which has taken place. Young people from Christian homes are brought up in the old framework. In time they become confused because they do not understand the alternatives with which they are being presented. Confusion becomes bewilderment, and before long they are overwhelmed. This is unhappily true not only of young people, but of many pastors, Christian educators, evangelists and missionaries as well."[8]

Those words, written in 1968, are among the most prophetic ever penned outside of the Scriptures. Frances Schaeffer saw the problem, warned us of the problem, and (sadly) was ignored by far too many in the church. I am no prophet. I'd have to be utterly blind, however, not to see the impact that generations of presenting an unsound understanding of truth and knowledge have had on our country, and on the church.

That problem is exacerbated by a failure of those in church leadership to insist, and yes, I mean insist, that the people who attend our local evangelical churches continue in the important discipline of "renewing their minds."[9] Once we stop our efforts to renew our minds, we soon lose our way. I will turn my attention more fully to this in the final chapter.

Secondly, it is crucial for us to understand that education by its very nature is never neutral in how it perceives the world and in its instruction on how individuals are to live in the world. Education is value-laden; it is not neutral. In fact, the idea of an unfailingly objective education devoid of the influence of any personal belief, is largely a fantasy. Without question, some teachers and professors make an attempt at neutrality, but who we are and what we believe cannot long stay hidden in any class-room anywhere.

In one of the most insightful, and sadly ignored, books written in the last forty years, the authors of *Disestablishment a Second Time* made this important observation: "The fundamental dilemma of a majoritarian, monopolistic educational structure is plain. Since education would always be religious (never neutral) in some form, whether Protestant, Catholic, secular, or something else, a majoritarian system would always offend the religious conscience of those in the majority."[10]

That is exactly the goal Jefferson was pursuing through a uniform, public system of education. The goal was to eradicate the differences that defined people and replace those differences with a common understanding of "the way things are supposed to be." Jefferson's vision fired the imagination of a young man from the state of Massachusetts who did more to shape our educational system than perhaps anyone until John Dewey in the 20th century. His name: Horace Mann, and he has rightfully been called the father of American public education. To him and that infamous deal with the devil I now turn my attention.

## The Awful Price of Bigotry

Bigotry exists. It is an ugly expression of our fallen nature. I've been guilty of it. And if you are honest, so have you. Bigotry is always unhealthy, like a bad cold, but it can become far more destructive, much like the COVID-19 virus that is sweeping our country and threatening the very fabric of our social and economic life. That is the kind of bigotry that led to the current monopolistic system of publicly funded schools in the USA today.

To understand the origins of our existing system, we have to put ourselves into another time. We have to see, as the founders of our country saw, the terrible religious conflicts that had for centuries torn Europe apart. Catholics hated Protestants. Protestants hated Catholics. And both hated those who became known as the Non-conformists, as Baptists and Anabaptists and other groups that would not "conform" to the theological norms in power at the time were called.

The Pilgrims and Puritans were nonconformists, as were the Quakers who founded the colony of Pennsylvania. These were groups that chose to flee the Old World for the New World in search of religious freedom. These, and their descendants and their religious cobelligerents, were the ones for whom the first amendment to the constitution was written—designed to ensure that America, these United States, would be the first major country in the Western world to have freedom of religion and religious expression. In America there was to be no state-sponsored, state-funded religion.

That is not to say that there were not favored religious groups and disfavored religious groups in America at the time. Without question, a kind of watered-down, lowest-common-denominator Protestantism was the favored religious expression. Equally without a doubt, Judaism and Roman Catholicism, while tolerated at some level, were certainly not favored. As Lawrence Cremin, a leading educational historian, has noted,

> The vernaculars of American education sought to provide a sense of community for a people who were increasing in numbers, diversifying in origin, and insistently mobile. Granting that the *paideia* was never static, and that it varied significantly from place to place, I believe it may be fairly characterized as a Christian paideia that united the symbols of Protestantism, the values of the New Testament, *Poor Richard's Almanac*, the Federalist Papers, and the aspirations asserted on the great seal.[11]

This position was easy to embrace because the early republic, to a large extent, was populated by a homogenous people who were generally characterized by a Protestant worldview. Thus, despite our repudiation of a state-sponsored, state-funded church, the various Protestant groups were willing to embrace a kind of alternative to a formal state church—the common school, a place where the specifics of Protestant theology might not be taught, but a place where basic Protestant values and beliefs would shape all instruction.

In one sense, therefore, the emerging American common school system became a de facto state religion, "taking over one of the basic responsibilities that traditionally was always assumed by an established church. In this sense the public-school system of the United States is its established church."[12] I know that statement may sound a bit out there, but please read on.

This modified state church was a problem that remained beneath the surface of our country until the 1840s, when masses of Irish citizens began immigrating to the United States during what has become known as the great Irish Potato Famine. Those immigrants, virtually all Catholic, made their way primarily to two cities, New York and Boston. The response of America's Protestant majority was ugly. As one whose ancestors were both Irish and Jewish, I am particularly sensitive to that historical reality.[13]

Sadly, as I will attempt to demonstrate, that prejudice, that bigotry, opened the door to a devil's bargain between educational reformers of the day, led by Horace Mann, and Protestant politicians and church leaders.

## The Devil Is in the Details.

Horace Mann has been called the father of public education. He was certainly not alone in his efforts, but without question the establishment of a common school system in the state of Massachusetts came about largely as a result of his tireless efforts. His desires in this regard were so strong that one author noted, "If the American public-school movement took on the tone of a religious crusade after Mann became secretary of the Board of Education, it was because Mann himself saw it as a religious crusade."[14]

Mann, like Jefferson before him, saw the public system as a means to instill the codes of conduct, social values, and occupational skills necessary to preserve a Protestant middle-class ethic in an increasingly industrial society.[15] Mann had powerful political allies in this endeavor, in the persons of Daniel Webster and Edward Everett, two influential senators. These men, staunch Whigs (the anti-immigration party of the day), were alarmed at the influx of immigrants, especially Irish Catholics, to this country. They saw a public system of state-supported schools as the best means available to inculcate the American ethic (which, as I have previously pointed out, was a largely Protestant ethic) into these people. As the authors of *Disestablishment a Second Time* put it, "The role of the good teacher was to inculcate 'correct doctrine' lest the illiterate, poor, and foreign born become a threat to the established institutions and way of life."[16]

While Mann was religious, his beliefs were largely aligned with Jefferson—both were deists—meaning that they did not believe in a personal God who engaged in human affairs.[17] They both believed, however, in a Protestant moral ethic, and they both equally despised the Roman Catholic Church and Calvinism. The goal for Mann, therefore, as noted earlier, was to use the common schools of Boston and New York as the means to inculcate the Protestant worldview, though not the particulars of the various Protestant belief systems, into the students who attended, while at the same time disenfranchising the Roman Catholic Church by prohibiting public funding for schools sponsored by the Catholic dioceses of first Boston and then New York.

Under this arrangement the common schools, though clearly Protestant in nature, were declared to be nonsectarian, meaning that they did not represent a specific denomination. Catholic schools were, however, declared to be sectarian in nature because they, of course, represented a specific denomination, the Roman Catholic Church. As a consequence, the various Catholic dioceses were denied funding for their schools. They were not denied the freedom to form their own schools, of course, but they had to fund their own schools apart from "public" dollars.

So, why does this matter to us today? It matters because the system that our Protestant forefathers approved and applauded in the 1840s is being used to disenfranchise evangelical Christians today. That was the bargain we made then, and now Mr. Scratch has come calling.

This approach to funding schools in America is now so ingrained in our public consciousness that few people ever raise a question about how we got here. It's just the way it is. In fact, as most people will say, "It's because the Constitution requires the separation of church and state." That understanding of the first amendment is, of course, simply not correct. What the first amendment prohibits is the establishment of a particular state-sponsored and state-funded church. Sadly, the result of that misunderstanding has actually led to the establishment of a de facto state church in the form of the American public-school system.

If, as I believe, all education is essentially religious, when that word is properly understood, then no education can be considered neutral. That was true in the 1840s when the Protestant worldview predominated, and it is true in the 2020s as a secular worldview predominates. In both cases, the publicly funded school system becomes a place where a particular worldview forms the basis for all instruction and other worldviews are banished from the marketplace of ideas. Such a system was inappropriate in the 1840s, and it is equally inappropriate today.

By the way, the USA is one of the few Western-style democracies that chooses to fund education the way it does. In most countries that operate under some form of Western-style democracy, tax funds follow the student to whatever school their parents choose. They can attend a school guided by Marie Montessori's philosophy or a Waldorf School or a Catholic school or a Protestant school or virtually any kind of school as long as those schools can demonstrate that all students are learning essential content and developing the skills necessary to navigate the modern world.

In a country that has historically disapproved of monopolies, it continues to astonish me that we in the U.S. have accepted a public-school monopoly that creates a false distinction between private education and public education. All education is public in the sense that all schools work to prepare children for life in and service to the public good. To deny funding for those schools that have been arbitrarily labeled "sectarian" or "private" is fundamentally in conflict with our values as Americans.

It isn't, however, in conflict with the same kind of political and cultural authorities that established our current flawed funding system in the 1840s. Those powerful groups will, and do, fight every effort to address the inadequacies and unfairness of our current approach to funding schools. It is time for the church in the USA to take a stand on the issue and perhaps in some small way rectify the errors of our past. It is time for the church in the USA to reassert its authority to educate its children and young people as part of its disciple-making mandate.

## For Reflection

1. For Thomas Jefferson and Horace Mann, two key individuals behind the development of what became known as the "common school" in America, the foundation for education was human reason. For the followers of Jesus Christ the foundation is more than human reason alone. How would those differing approaches shape the education of children?

2. If it is true that reason untethered from true truth tends to lead people away from God, what can we learn about the consequences of this approach from a study of Romans 1:18–23?

3. According to the Scriptures, why is reason an inadequate starting place for the education of our children?

4. If, as the authors of *Disestablishment a Second Time* argue, no education is ever truly a completely objective activity, why have "private" faith-based schools been excluded from public funding? Why not allow all schools to receive public funding? What impact has this policy had on how we educate our children in the USA?

Chapter 11

## Where Do We Go From Here?

One of the most iconic characters in children's literature is Mary Poppins, whose exploits are explored over the course of nine books authored by P. L. Travers. Mary, as portrayed by Travers, is a most remarkable mix of strict authoritarian and magical, mystical adventurer who quickly wins the hearts of the Banks children: Jane, Michael, and the twins, John and Barbara.

For the 1964 film adaptation of the first Mary Poppins book, the musical brothers Robert and Richard Sherman composed some memorable music and lyrics to help tell the story. Among the most unforgettable was a little ditty titled "A Spoonful of Sugar." The origin of that song is fascinating.

After receiving instructions from Walt Disney himself to compose something catchy to help advance the narrative of a particular scene, Robert Sherman, the primary lyricist of the two brothers, had arrived home after a fruitless day of trying to come up with an idea. As he walked in the door that evening his wife, Joyce, informed him that the children had gotten their polio vaccine that day. Thinking his children had received a shot, he asked one of them if it hurt.

His son responded that the medicine had been put on a cube of sugar and that he had swallowed it with no pain. As is often the case with a gifted writer, Robert realized that he had just been given the inspiration for a song. After sharing the idea with his brother, Richard put melody to the lyric Robert had written, and a wonderful show tune was born.

I tell that story for a simple reason. I do understand that flavoring strong medicine can indeed make it easier to take. There are times, however, when we just have to take the medicine even when it tastes bad because if we don't, we stay sick or perhaps we die. I was one of those children who stood in a long line to receive a polio vaccine as a young child. In fact, like nearly all children of my age, we ended up receiving three shots. They all hurt.

As Professor David Oshinsky reminds us, polio was an insidious childhood disease that came like clockwork each summer during the middle years of the 20th century, killing thousands and crippling many more."[1] It's the disease that put Franklin Roosevelt into a wheelchair for much of his life. It is the disease that, until Jonas Salk created his famous vaccine, put fear into the hearts of millions of American parents and sorrow into uncounted thousands of those same hearts.

So, when the vaccine became available, millions of parents and children endured long lines without complaint, despite the pain associated with receiving the vaccine. It was clear to all that the hours spent in line and a bit of minor discomfort were a small price to pay for a healthy child.

I am hoping that perhaps you will afford me the same grace as I write this concluding chapter. I wish there were some kind of sweetener to add to what might be perceived as some pretty strong language. All I can offer, however, is a vision of a better, healthier future than the one currently staring us in the face.

The apostle Paul encourages us to always speak the truth in love. But doing so can still sting. Perhaps that is why the author of the Old Testament book of Proverbs reminds us, "Better is open rebuke than hidden love. Faithful are the wounds of a friend, profuse are the kisses of an enemy" (Proverbs 27:5–6). I see that as my role in this book, and particularly in this chapter. It's time to speak truth in love, and truth to power.

In some ways I feel like a doctor who has performed an examination, having looked at all of the relevant test results, and must now give his patient a diagnosis and offer a suggested treatment protocol. And sadly, sugar isn't going to make things any easier. This is a malignant disease that left untreated will cause great harm—already has caused great harm. I wish it wasn't so, but the best evidence out there suggests it is time to take radical action.

The patient can, of course, choose not to follow the advice of a doctor. Failure to act won't, however, change what is taking place inside the body. As would be true of most doctors, I'm open to a different course of action, but only if there is a better possible outcome at the end. Wishing and hoping and asserting aren't, however, a sufficient framework for action. We must go where the evidence leads us. In this case I believe that the evidence is best found in the Scriptures, coupled with key lessons from history and quality research.

I hope that thus far I have provided key evidence from Scripture along with some sound historical insight and cultural research. In this chapter I want to add a bit more of all three to describe a way forward.

## Step 1: It's Time to Admit That the Problem Is Real and Growing.

I have a fairly bulging collection (efiles, of course) of articles on the current growing exodus of young people from the church. The reasons for that exodus and the growing tide of that exodus have become increasingly clear over the last few years.

It has been argued in many articles I have read that this recent exodus is nothing new. Young people have often left the church only to return as they settle down, get married, and start a family. That explanation doesn't seem to get much support from the current research, however. As Daniel Cox and Amelia Thompson-DeVeaux observe in a recent fivethirtyeight article, "For a long time . . . it wasn't clear whether this youthful defection from religion would be temporary or permanent. It seemed possible that as millennials grew older, at least some would return to a more traditional religious life. But there's mounting evidence that today's younger generations may be leaving religion for good."[2]

John Stonestreet echoes that finding on his Colson Center BreakPoint Daily post of February 25, 2020. What he has to say should cause every parent and pastor to pause and ponder. He writes, "According to Pew Research four in ten Americans between the ages of 23–38 now say they are religiously unaffiliated. This is the biggest drop in religiosity between generations ever recorded. While part of the hemorrhaging is explained by the forty-year decline in mainline Protestant bodies, evangelicals are not off the hook. We cannot say that conservative theology, in and of itself, is enough to shrink-proof your church. The Southern Baptist Convention, for example, America's largest evangelical denomination, just hit a 30-year membership low."[3]

I am aware that there are those that dismiss these findings as unpersuasive or as missing all of the good things that are happening among young people today. Good, however, is a relative thing. That young people show up to serve meals at a homeless shelter is, of course, a good thing. We should certainly applaud that kind of public service. The deeper question, and the one we seem unwilling to ask, is this: What is shaping their thinking, behavior, and view of the world as they perform those acts?

As I detailed in chapter 6, behavior always emerges from what we value, and what we value is built upon what we believe to be true. Without a proper worldview, even good deeds do not always represent a truly biblical understanding of the world and our role in that world.

While it is time to admit that the news is bad ("We really are losing a generation of young churchgoers, and they're probably not coming back—at least not if we stay our present course"[4]) there is also good news—news that supports the foundational claims of this book.

"The good news: We now know with even greater clarity the difference parents make, and we can apply that with members of Generation Z (or any generation for that matter). Parents who prioritize church as a central part of their family life, who teach their children to take Christianity seriously, and who encourage them to marry fellow believers, have the best chance of seeing not only their children but also their grandchildren in the pews beside them."[5]

Given current cultural realities and the admonition of Scripture, however, it is time to recognize that even the most diligent of parents need partners in fulfilling their responsibility to "bring up their children in the *paideia* of Christ." Not only can't it be done alone, it shouldn't be done alone.

There is more good news, however, good news based on sound research. "In 2007 Cardus, a Canadian think tank and research group, hosted a symposium of 37 leaders, including representation from virtually all Christian school groups in North America. They examined these questions:

- Is Christian education having the lasting impact our schools say it has?
- And, if so, how do we know?

Following the symposium, Cardus launched a million-dollar research project. The project was led by Ray Pennings, senior fellow and director of research at Cardus."[6]

So, what were the results of that extensive research? In its executive summary, the Cardus Education Survey states the following:

> In contrast to the popular stereotypes portraying Christian schools as promoting a socially fragmented, anti-intellectual, politically radical, militantly right-winged lifestyle, this comprehensive study reveals a very different picture of the Christian school graduate. Compared to their public school, Catholic school, and non-religious private school peers, Protestant Christian School graduates are uniquely compliant, generous, outwardly-focused individuals who stabilize their

communities by the uncommon commitment to their families, their churches, and larger society.[7]

Christian schooling does make a remarkable difference, and it is time that pastors and parents put aside their personal biases to at least consider the observations from such credible research. Obviously, the impact is not equal in the lives of every student for the reasons I mentioned in an earlier chapter. The impact is, however, clear and measurable.

## Step 2: It's Time to Change Tactics.

If the history of warfare teaches us anything, it's that when technology changes, tactics must adjust in response. Failure to do so always ends in greater, unnecessary casualties. Iron beat bronze, and then steel beat iron. The wheeled chariot certainly had an advantage over foot soldiers. The English longbow was a far better weapon, especially at long range, than the French crossbow. Gunpowder was superior to the longbow, tanks and machine guns overwhelmed horse cavalry, and airpower proved more deadly than ground troops. You adapt, adopt, or die.

We find ourselves at just such a crossroads in our calling to make disciples. Certainly, some things never change. The weapons of our warfare, for example, haven't changed. Ephesians 6 still matters, as does the life-on-life component that marked the ministry of our Lord and of the apostles. For those things there are no substitutes.

In saying that, however, if we aren't careful, we miss something. We miss the heart of what Jesus did, what Paul did, what so many of the great teachers of the church did and still do. And more dangerously, we miss how much of their strategy is absent in today's church.

For one thing, we sorely overlook the daily, incarnational aspect of their ministries. I spent considerable time addressing that in an earlier chapter. I return to that topic here because I believe it is our failure to grasp the importance of that single factor that is at the heart of our current difficulties.

We are too easily seduced by past methodologies and current technology. We somehow believe, for example, that putting a large group of people in a room together to hear a message from a gifted teacher is sufficient to the task of making disciples who obey all that Christ demanded of us. That is a fantasy. It may be a viable strategy for evangelism. It is not, however, the singular way forward if our goal is to make disciples who will actually live out in their daily lives what Christ taught in His daily life. It is the equivalent to what we in education refer to as the "sage on the stage."

I know about being a sage on the stage. I've served in that capacity at hundreds of conferences throughout the years. It is an efficient way to get content out there. It is a terrible methodology, however, if your goal is to help people make sense of that content. Except in the rarest of situations, it will never lead to the kind of actions by an individual or within an organization that change things for the better.

As Dr. Charlie Phillips of the McClellan Foundation noted in a private conversation, "School leaders don't need more information so much as they need longitudinal coaching."[8] By longitudinal coaching Dr. Phillips meant ongoing conversation about specific issues over a long period of time with someone who has a sufficient grasp of key information so as to be truly helpful. Content matters. Figuring out how best to employ that content in the day-to-day realities of life is equally important, and it is a key component sorely lacking in our approach to disciple making in the 21st century.

The typical response to that observation goes something like this: "That is what parents are supposed to do. The pastor's job or the youth pastor's job is to get the content out there. The parents' responsibility is to help their children see the best way to employ that content in their everyday life."

Well, in an agrarian world such as we find in Deuteronomy 6, that approach held some promise. In a modern world in which parents and children are seldom in the same place at the same time for any length of time, that just won't work, and it hasn't worked for a very long time. The people our children spend the most amount of time with will have the most impact on their lives. If I had been dependent on what my parents had to teach me about God's Word and how His Word should shape my life, I would have been lost.

Hopefully that makes some sense to you. Kids need more than words, no matter how clever those words might be, no matter how those words have been enhanced by technology. An ancient observer of human nature understood this far better than it seems we do today when he wrote, "By mere words a servant is not disciplined, for though he understands, he will not respond."[9]

That reality might help explain why we are told that the apostles were daily teaching in households all over the city of Jerusalem, or why the ministry of the apostle Paul was characterized by daily teaching, or why the writer of Hebrews not only encouraged people to gather on a regular basis but also to "consider how to stir up one another to love and good works"[10] with the content under consideration. Information that doesn't change how we behave is actually pretty useless. Sadly, the likelihood that information will remain useless remains pretty high unless there is ongoing, frequent encouragement to act on what we are learning.

There may have been a time when showing up for a Sunday sermon or a weekly youth meeting was a sufficient tactic, but if it ever was it no longer is. That is especially the case if, and here the medicine might sting a little, the content is less than stellar, which is, unfortunately, too often true in the church today.

The late J. P. Moreland addressed the importance of quality content: "If a culture reaches the point where Christian claims are not even a part of its plausibility structure [a person's plausibility structure is the set of ideas the person either is or is not willing to entertain as possibly true], fewer and fewer people will be able to entertain the possibility that they might be true."[11]

How close do you think we are to that reality at present? I think that day has been upon us for quite a few years now. What we should be asking is not how close are we to that reality in our culture, but how close to that reality are we in "the church." Given what we are learning from the research, I would say far too many of our young people have decided that what they hear in church is just not all that plausible. And I would argue that has become the case because we've done a poor job with both content and incarnation. Until that changes, the current trend of walking away from the church will only accelerate.

Christian schooling, whether in a homeschool setting, in a traditional classroom setting, or in a formal, rigorous program in a local church, when done right (which sadly is not always the case), is without question the best and most biblically appropriate way to address the issues I have presented. That brings me to step three in this process.

## Step 3: It's Time to Decide.

My friend Mickey Bowden would often say, "The worst thing you can do to a child is to systematically expose them to error, especially when they are not equipped to discern the difference between truth and error." He is right. Yet as a whole that is exactly what the church has chosen to do in supporting our contemporary, monopolistic, secular, publicly funded school system.

I'll get to why the church has chosen to do this in a moment. First, however, I want to emphasize something I said in the last chapter. The idea that emerged in the early years of our new republic to work toward providing a quality education to all children and young people was, and remains, a good and worthy goal. No one benefits from large-scale ignorance except a tyrant.

The idea was a noble one. The execution has, however, been less than stellar in some pretty notable ways. One problem has been our choice to fund education primarily through property taxes. This is a huge issue and has caused significant disparities in funding school districts around the country. Put simply, suburban school districts, in which property values tend to be high, generally have greater levels of funding than do inner-city urban school districts, even when state money is added. This is a serious problem, but is not the focus of this book.

The greater problem, one that is virtually ignored by most people, is the monopolistic nature of our educational system. That did not happen by accident. Remember from the preceding chapter that one of the primary goals of those early champions of the "common school" was to create a graduate who understood and embraced the "common" values that would make someone a model citizen of the new nation.

Recall as well that those common values were at one point a kind of lowest common denominator Protestantism. Thus, it became a key mission of those early common schools to take the children of the Irish immigrants flooding into New York City and Boston, and "crush them into the mold" of the new American citizen, meaning those children would in time come to embrace a Protestant belief system. Understandably many of those early Irish Catholic immigrant parents did not respond well to such a plan. I can't fault them for their response.

You see, what was actually happening was not just the development of a common school system but also, though less noticeably, the establishment of a state-sponsored quasi-church, one with a very specific theological framework. While watered down, it was still decidedly Protestant, and decidedly hostile to other worldviews. If you doubt that observation, consider small-town America of the 19th and early-20th centuries. What was the single common community gathering place? Was it the local Baptist church or the local Presbyterian church or the local Methodist church or the local Catholic parish? No, it was the local public school, primarily the high school where athletic events took place.[12]

Once in place, that monopolistic system became the seedbed for what was to replace the old theistic world, with a view as hostile to the Protestant Christian faith as the Protestants had been to Catholics, Jews, and many other faiths.

The flaw in the system was not the desire to provide a quality education to every child. Rather, it was the one-size-fits-all structure that became a tool in the hands of whoever held the greatest control over the content of the current cultural worldview at any time. It was a tool that would be used, as it had been in the past, to force conformity on virtually every key issue of the day. We see exactly that in the current unrelenting efforts in our schools to recast our entire understanding of human sexuality.

Thus, we find ourselves today in exactly the same place as those mid-19th-century Catholics. In a very real sense, we, like they, must sit by and watch our children indoctrinated into a worldview that clashes with our own. And indoctrination is not too strong a word. Schooling is certainly about teaching kids to read. The question is not whether a kid should read. The question is what should they be reading and who will provide guidance as they read. The question is not whether they should learn to compute. The question that should be asked is to what end should they learn to compute. The same could be said of science and history and every other discipline students are asked to learn in school.

Until that monopoly can be overthrown, we, speaking of those who identify as followers of Jesus Christ, have two options. The first is to leave our children in an environment that is becoming more openly hostile to what we believe to be true and then do our best to push back against the daily barrage of false truth claims in school and in the media. As the research is clearly telling us, however, that strategy doesn't seem to be working if we want our kids to embrace the gospel and live out its implications in their lives.

The second option, one that many Christian parents have chosen, is to seek a different approach to the education of their children. For some, that different approach is homeschooling. Homeschooling, and not just among Christian families, is one of the fastest-growing educational sectors in our country. The continual development and refinement of online curriculum has made this option increasingly more accessible to families. In spite of its growth, however, homeschooling and online schooling only make up a small percentage of students in the USA.

The vast majority of parents who seek an alternative to the public-school system will choose some kind of private or faith-based school. The cost of making that choice, however, is substantial, putting such an option beyond the reach of many of the people who are dissatisfied with either the academic quality of the school their child attends or with the worldview approach of the school their child attends—or in many cases, both reasons.

For many families with students enrolled in failing urban schools, the rise of charter schools has provided a beacon of hope. Interestingly, however, despite the fact that charter schools are by law "public" schools, the opposition to charters by the two main teacher unions has been unrelenting, bitter, and sadly has, in many cases, been alarmingly dishonest.[13] That fact alone should give all of us pause as to the real intentions of the educational establishment in our country.

Parents who choose either a secular private school or a faith-based school are faced with paying tuition that in many cases can be substantial. Writing a monthly tuition check is, however, like paying a double tax, something most people can ill afford. It is an unfair system for the same reason that a monopoly is unfair; it leaves the customer at the mercy of a single provider.

Our representatives in Washington are quick to strike out against any appearance of a monopoly in the marketplace, but are, for the most part, avid supporters of the current publicly funded secular school system. I, for one, find that both interesting and infuriating.

Where does all I have had to say thus far in this book leave us as the Body of Christ? As my action step 3 suggests, I believe it's time for us to make a choice. We can choose to embrace the current system, or we can choose to embrace a better system, and by better, I mean a system more aligned with the teaching of Scripture. It is, however, time to decide. Turning a blind eye to our current reality will have growing and disastrous consequences for the body of Christ here and around the world.

There are those in the church, in fact there are many in the church, who would say, "Alan, the decision about the education of children is one each family must make according to their own conscience." My response to that familiar statement is twofold. First, I would argue that my conscience, or your conscience, as a follower of Jesus Christ, can only be a reliable guide when it is informed by the Scriptures. When it comes to the issue of education, I strongly believe that the Scriptures have played virtually no role in the current conversation.

Second, I would argue that the church is a body made up of individual parts that are and must be fully connected to and fully dependent upon every other member of the body. The church is not simply a collection of individuals who might or might not decide to show up at a particular location on a Sunday morning or a Saturday night or whenever. We have obligations to one another, obligations that are clearly enumerated and described in the New Testament Scriptures, obligations that make it clear that we are dependent upon one another for the decisions we make and the actions that we take.

## A Time to Be Counter-Cultural

I am well aware that what I have briefly described above is in conflict with our prevailing cultural point of view here in the USA and in many other places around the world. Indeed, in many places, support for the local public school is almost seen as a patriotic statement.

If Christians are to be anything, however, we are certainly called to be counter-cultural, and while we are to exercise wise citizenship wherever in the world we live, we must never forget that we are, first and foremost, citizens of another realm. Sadly, however, counter-cultural as it would have been understood in Scripture is not something descriptive of the evangelical church today.

No one I have read over the years has captured this concept more clearly than John Stott in his book aptly titled *Christian Counter-Culture: The Message of the Sermon on the Mount.* I'm including a lengthy portion of the first chapter from that book because I believe the message is critical to us today as it relates to how we must view our obligations as the people of God in a world that is increasingly antagonistic to what we have been called to be and do.

> For insofar as the church is conformed to the world, and the two communities appear to the onlooker to be merely two versions of the same thing, the church is contradicting its true identity. No comment could be more hurtful to the Christian than the words, "But you are no different from anybody else."

> For the essential theme of the whole Bible from beginning to end is that God's historical purpose is to call out a people for himself; that this people is a "holy" people, set apart from the world to belong to him and to obey him; and that its vocation is to be true to its identity, that is, to be "holy" or "different" in all its outlook and behavior.

This is how God put it to the people of Israel soon after he had rescued them from their Egyptian slavery and made them his special people by covenant: "I am the Lord your God. You shall not do as they do in the land of Egypt, where you dwelt, and you shall not do as they do in the land of Canaan, to which I am bringing you. You shall not walk in their statutes. You shall do my ordinances and keep my statutes and walk in them. I am the Lord your God."

This appeal of God to his people, it will be noted, began and ended with the statement that he was the Lord their God. It was because he was their covenant God, and because they were his special people, that they were to be different from everybody else. They were to follow his commandments and not take their lead from the standards of those around them.

Sadly, as Stott continues,

Throughout the centuries which followed, the people of Israel kept forgetting their uniqueness as the people of God. Although in Balaam's words they were "a people dwelling alone, and not reckoning itself among the nations," yet in practice they kept becoming assimilated to the people around them: "They mingled with the nations and learned to do as they did."[14]

That is, to my observation, especially in the realms of politics, education, and our focus on wealth and comfort, exactly where the church finds itself today. Now I am not suggesting that we take up residence in some rural corner of the world as have the Amish. Doing so misses the point that we also serve as salt and light.

Serving as salt and light does not, however, require conformity to the culture. In fact, the opposite is true. (See Matthew 5:13.) We certainly have ample evidence of that in both the Scripture and in history. The list of people who shook the world while remaining true to God's calling, people who refused to give in to the siren song of the prevailing culture, is long.

I was reminded of this most recently while reading Eric Metaxas' superb biography of William Wilberforce. Wilberforce was the great member of the English Parliament who spearheaded the effort to abolish the slave trade and slavery itself throughout the English empire, and did so at great personal cost. It is one of the most inspiring stories I have ever read, as well as one of the most instructive. While Wilberforce worked within the political structure of the day, he never yielded to the prevailing cultural forces of his day. We need more men and women like that today. The current secular public-school system is not, however, the soil from which those kinds of people will be nourished and grown, and it never will be. We need different soil and a different system if we ever hope to change the world in which we currently dwell.

A major obstacle to reshaping the American system of education is money. Because the system is a monopoly jealously guarded by the teacher unions and their political allies in government, we will need to continue outside of the current system efforts. To do that in a way that will make a truly Christ-centered education available to all who desire such an education will require far greater engagement from evangelical churches all across the country and around the world—and a much greater financial and programmatic commitment from those churches—than is the current reality.

## So, What's the Problem?

So, what keeps the church from coming together for this purpose? First of all, too few church leaders and too few parents see the need. My purpose in writing this book is to perhaps spark a conversation that might change that reality.

Secondly, the church in America and in much of the world seems to be focused on a different set of priorities, particularly evangelism or social justice. Neither focus is wrong. Both, however, miss key points. Neither activity should be separated from the specific and direct mission given us by our Lord to make disciples. In fact, both activities are fully dependent upon fulfillment of that commission.

If all we do is make spiritual babies, which is the unfortunate result of much evangelistic effort in the world today, then the church is destined to remain vulnerable and ineffective. How often have you heard it said that 80% of the work done in a church is done by 20% of the people or that 80% of the giving in a church is done by 20% of the people? Why do you think that is true? My guess is that the statistic is true because many of that 80% in the typical evangelical church remain in spiritual infancy. And worse, we have just come to accept that reality as normal.

It also explains why so few American Christians or churches are willing to be involved in the difficult work that serving as real salt and light requires of us. We would rather, it seems, put our money into building bigger and better places to gather while in turn creating huge infrastructure costs just to keep the doors open. It's not a good look in this broken world, and it certainly isn't a wise use of the resources we have been given.

Strong words, I know. However, while you may disagree with my definition of and prescription for making disciples, I can't imagine that as a follower of Jesus Christ you could come to any other conclusion. If nothing else, I would hope you would agree that we live in perilous times and that life as usual is not a good response.

## Step 4: It's Time to Serve as Real Salt and Light.

I know that some of my readers think that I am suggesting an abandonment of the public schools. I'm not suggesting that at all. In fact, I see America's public schools as one of the most desperate mission fields in the world. Where error abounds, darkness descends. Nowhere is that more true than in the current secular school system in the USA and many other places around the world.

I'm not making an argument to abandon the public schools; rather, I'm making an argument for engaging the public schools, but doing so with people who are prepared for and equipped to undertake that engagement. The vast majority of our children and young people do not fit that description. To believe otherwise is naïve, and dangerous for them. Once again, the research is making that clearer and clearer every day.

There are, however, ways to pursue purposeful engagement that can make a difference. All of what I am about to suggest is, however, becoming increasingly difficult to accomplish because of the growing restrictions regarding "religious" speech on public-school campuses. Yes, I know that certain student-led actions receive less scrutiny from school officials, but the overall climate on most public-school campuses is decidedly and diametrically opposed to the work of the gospel. There are nonetheless three areas that are still open to our efforts to make a difference.

The first of those areas are the teachers and administrators in public schools who are Christ-followers. Note I didn't say "Christian" teachers. There is a huge gap between claiming to be a "Christian" (which a huge percentage of Americans claim) and being a faithful, maturing follower of the Christ of Scripture. Some teachers are actually quite successful in their "missionary" efforts. Much could be learned when their experiences are shared with other teachers. There are even organizations that exist for the very purpose of encouraging and equipping public-school teachers to be more effective in their efforts to bring the gospel into the classroom and beyond.[15]

Sadly, the deepening darkness enveloping so much of the current academy is making it increasingly difficult for teachers of faith to speak out. My evidence is only anecdotal, but I continually hear stories of teachers who are saying, "I just can't take it anymore." That is tragic but understandable. Thus, it is crucial for the church to be unrelenting in its support for those teachers who have chosen the American public-school system as their mission field. Those teachers should be supported in much the same way that other missionaries are supported.

Sadly, however, not all teachers view their work as an opportunity to serve God's kingdom in a difficult place. For many it is a job for which they are being paid. That is an unfortunate reality, but it is a reality. Perhaps it might make sense for churches to help teachers see their role in a more biblical light and provide equipping for how they could be better at their role of missionary.

Secondly, I believe that the body of Christ should find ways to recruit volunteers and make them available to public schools in their area. This would especially be helpful for inner-city urban schools and for schools in poorer districts.

I would not just descend on local schools. I would first want to sit down with the on-site leaders of those schools and ask this simple question: What could we as a church do to help you and your students? Let them identify the needs and let them suggest the best strategies. You are coming to them, not to rescue them, but to join them in a partnership.

Those leaders will, of course, remind any volunteer of the limitations imposed by federal, state, and local regulations regarding attempts to introduce religion into any activity. As a volunteer, it is imperative that you acknowledge and honor those regulations.

The opportunity a volunteer would have, however, is the power of incarnation, the life-on-life opportunity to model the grace of God. Over time, if you are consistent in your efforts to reflect Christ accurately, it is highly likely that the students whom you may be tutoring or mentoring will start asking you questions. There are no regulations, at least none of which I am aware, against responding graciously and in a noncoercive manner to those questions. Even so, I would still suggest that a conversation with the leadership of the school would make sense. One of the most powerful elements of true biblical faith is service done in love. We forget that to our peril.

Thirdly, we can work diligently toward dismantling our current monopolistic system of education and the funding formula that sustains that flawed system. In many Western-style democracies, educational funds follow the student. If parents choose to send their children to a local Catholic school, educational funds follow them to that school. If they choose to send them to a local Montessori school, educational funds follow them to that school. The same would be true should they choose a STEM-focused school or a Christian classical school or a fine-arts-focused school designed around a Christian worldview.

Having the education revenue follow the student is a far better approach than the current command-and-control approach that is condemning so many students to an inferior education and many others to what amounts to indoctrination into whatever current cultural fad is viewed as enlightened. And, as noted earlier, this is not some radical idea. Rather, it is common practice in much of the world.

So why don't we even consider such an approach in our country? I'll suggest two reasons. First, of all, though I suspect many reading this book and certainly most people out there don't agree with my assessment, the American public school is, and always has been, in many ways a state quasi-church. As Americans we are free to believe what we want to believe so long as what we believe stays within the realm of private belief.

Sadly, the church seems to have accepted this privatization of belief with little more than a whimper of protest. It's time for us to be a bit more robust in our response to this emasculation of the church. Belief is not just a private affair. Belief that does not manifest itself in daily life is dead.[16]

I wonder sometimes to what extent our fear of the blowback we will receive from the surrounding culture for standing firmly and publicly for righteousness disarms our efforts to do what is right. If that is where you find yourself, please read and ponder the following observation from one of the most godly and theologically sound men of the last generation.

The church is safe from vicious persecution at the hand of the secularists, as educated people have finished with stake-burning circuses and torture racks. No martyr's blood is shed in the secular west. So long as the church knows her place and remains quietly at peace on her modern reservation. Let the babes pray and sing and read their Bibles, continuing steadfastly in their intellectual retardation; the church's extinction will not come by sword or pillory, but by the quiet death of irrelevance. But let the church step off the reservation, let her penetrate once more the culture of the day and the . . . face of secularism will change from a benign smile to a savage snarl.[17]

That quote appeared in the book *Classical Apologetics*, published in 1984. Prophetic? I think so. When mainstream secular organizations like the Southern Poverty Law Center identifies individuals like John Stonestreet of the Colson Center, Eric Metaxas and organizations like the Alliance for Defending Freedom as purveyors of hate, we need to acknowledge that the smile has turned to a snarl.

I am not calling for a formal, organized response to those hateful allegations. I think that Eric Metaxas and John Stonestreet, as well as the highly competent attorneys at the Alliance for Defending Freedom, are quite capable of defending themselves. What I am hoping to encourage is an understanding that we need to get serious about the business of cultivating a generation of young people who know God's Word, who understand how best to live out that Word in our current cultural moment, and who will have the courage and grace to act on what they know to be true. Fail to do that well, and the snarl could quickly turn to something even more sinister.

Secondly, I would argue that our failure to challenge the current funding status quo will condemn millions of American children to an inferior education; inferior in a quality sense and equally inferior in a worldview sense. Doing so should be intolerable to us.

This is an opportunity for the white suburban church to link arms with African American parents, with Hispanic parents, and with parents of other minority groups in what I see as the greatest civil rights issue of our time. It is time—long past time, actually. As Moses proclaimed in Pharaoh's court, "Let my people go."

If you want more information about what is already being done to bring about a more just approach to funding schooling in the U.S., check out the information contained in this footnote.[18]

## A Final Plea

In the late 14th century, Gerard Groote, a young and wealthy man of Dutch descent, founded a monastic movement that became known as the Brethren of the Common Life. The Brethren established self-supporting communities within which those committed to its principles lived a simple Christian faith absent the kind of highly spiritualized rituals that were common in many monasteries in Europe at the time.

A primary focus of the Brethren was education, and they "spared no pains to obtain good masters [teachers] . . . for their schools, which became centers of spiritual and intellectual life."[19] Among those whom they trained or who were associated with them were men like Thomas à Kempis, Martin Luther, and the famous Dutch humanist Desiderius Erasmus. In fact, many of those who became leaders of the Protestant Reformation were students who studied in schools sponsored by the Brethren of the Common Life.

Indeed, among their chief aims were the education of a Christian elite and the promotion of the reading of devout literature.[20] Think of the Brethren as the Christian school movement of their day. Now think of the enormous impact of their efforts on the church and the world as a result of the Reformation.

Early in his book *To Change the World*, James Davidson Hunter observes, "To be Christian is to be obliged to engage the world, ensuring God's restorative purposes over all of life, individual and corporate, public and private. This is the mandate of creation."[21] He then spends the remainder of this book—336 pages including footnotes—unpacking the history of Christian engagement in the world since the death of Christ. There is much to learn from James Davidson Hunter in this book about our efforts to engage the culture—the good and the not-so-good.

Here is one of his key observations. "And as we've seen, the influence of the church grew as it penetrated the higher echelons of social life, and this was accomplished largely through its penetration and cooptation of the educational system."[22] What was to become the foundation of that system? Not surprisingly, the foundation was a Christian *paideia* that became "a preparatory school of Christian character."[23] So at another crucial point in the history of the church we see the emergence of what we would today call Christian schooling.

Let's go back a few centuries earlier in time to see another illustration of how faith-based schooling made a crucial difference at a critical time in the history of God's people.

Most of you who have been in church for any length of time can recall the story of the young Hebrew men who made such a mark on the Babylonian empire after the fall of Jerusalem. Daniel, Hananiah, Mishael, and Azariah (better known as Shadrach, Meshach, and Abednego) were of the tribe of Judah. They were taken from Jerusalem during the reign of Jehoiakim at the command of Nebuchadnezzar. The ruler of Babylon wanted to bring the cream of the crop, young men of nobility, good looks, skilled in wisdom, endowed with knowledge, understanding learning, so that they could serve their new sovereign.[24]

As part of their preparation to serve Nebuchadnezzar, those young men, who had already received an exceptional education in the court of Jehoiakim, were required to attend "graduate school" in Babylon. That graduate program would include courses in the literature and language of the Chaldeans. This would be a challenge because, "To begin to study Babylonian literature was to enter a completely alien thought-world."[25] Interestingly, at least to me, is the fact that, "the writer of Daniel implies no objection to the study of a polytheistic literature in which magic, sorcery, charms and astrology played a prominent part, though these had long been banned in Israel."[26]

To step into this world, however, required that "These young men from Jerusalem's court ... be secure in their knowledge of Yahweh [so that they would] be able to study this literature objectively without allowing it to undermine their faith. Evidently the work of Jeremiah, Zephaniah, and Habakkuk had not been in vain. In order to witness to their God in the Babylonian court they had to understand the cultural presuppositions of those around them, just as the Christian today must work hard at the religions and cultures amongst which he lives, if different thought-worlds [or as we might say today, different worldviews] are to meet."[27]

So, upon exploring the lives of those young Israelites who were forced into captivity and service to a pagan king, how well-prepared for the situation do you think they were? What kind of education would it take to equip them for such a difficult job? I would venture to say that they were remarkably well-prepared.

Each of those brief vignettes tells a similar story. Each illuminates a crucial hinge point in the history of God's work in this world. At each of those points God was preparing people to step onto the stage at a challenging moment in redemptive history. Yet in each case those individuals were well-prepared for the enormity of the task.

Our situation today is no different. We live in turbulent times, times that will require us to rigorously prepare our young people for life in that tempestuous world. So, my final question: Where is that kind of preparation most likely to happen? In the courts of Nebuchadnezzar? In the classrooms of the Greco-Roman philosophers? In the world of a fraying and highly speculative religious system? In the late-modern, "woke" classroom of 21st-century America?

Or is it most likely to happen in a place where godly people wrestle with the real issues of a world broken by sin and do so with an understanding that God's Word is the only real place to begin the conversation? You decide.

## For Reflection

1. How might an objective observer respond to the following statement? "According to Pew Research, four in ten Americans between the ages of 23 and 30 now say they are religiously unaffiliated. This is the biggest drop in religiosity between generations ever recorded." What questions might those observers ask? What further information might they seek?

2. Reread the conclusions of the 2007 Cardus study. Do those conclusions support your beliefs or challenge your beliefs? In what ways?

3. Given the rapid and radical changes in American culture, does the recent historic approach to discipling practiced in most churches still make sense? Why or why not? What would make sense?

4. Does our current monopolistic school system make sense in light of our cultural views on monopolies or in light of our increasingly diverse society? Why or why not?

5. In Scripture we are instructed to care for "the least of these." Does our monopolistic school system truly accomplish that goal? Is there a better way? What role should the church play in pursuing that better way?

6. What does it mean to be "counter-cultural" as John Stott describes that term in this chapter? How might thinking counter-culturally impact the way we educate our children?

7. How can Christians truly be salt and light when it comes to the education of children? Consider the examples given in this chapter. Add additional realistic ideas.

# Afterword

My work on this book draws to a close during two of the most troubling events in our history as a country. The first event was the COVID-19 pandemic. The second was the protests and riots that took place in the wake of George Floyd's death at the hands of police officers in Minneapolis, Minnesota. Both events revealed some rather troubling facts about life in 21st-century America. Both events resulted in great harm to individuals and communities throughout this country. And both events were in part driven by false narratives based on flawed research and ideas. It will take someone far more capable than I to unpack all of that. Hopefully someone will.

What has been a bit distressing to me personally during this moment is twofold:

- The underwhelming response of the church to these events.
- The lack of a theologically sound but culturally informed response to these events.

I'm sure that there have been many theologically sound and culturally adept articles and sermons written and delivered on both those topics, but what I have seen thus far leaves me wanting something of greater substance, greater depth, greater insight; something with more theological heft and less cultural wokeness. Frankly, much of it has seemed like pretty thin gruel, and tasteless at that.

As I reflected a bit on that observation, however, I came to a painful conclusion. Not only is the church failing to engage in real discipleship efforts of its children and young people, it seems to be failing equally in its efforts to disciple its adults, and for many of the same reasons. Discipleship is not an event. It is not a program. It is not a one-time, one-size-fits-all effort. It is, or should be, an ongoing effort to encourage and equip every Christ-follower with the knowledge, understanding, and wisdom necessary to live in a manner that honors Christ, reflects His person, and advances His purposes in the world. I am beginning to wonder if that is too much to ask. That is clearly the point the apostle Paul is making in his letter to the church in Ephesus.[1]

Paul repeatedly makes that point clear throughout his letters to the churches. For example, to the church at Rome he writes, "Do not be conformed to this world, but be transformed by the renewal of your mind, that by testing you may discern what is the will of God, what is good and acceptable and perfect."[2]

In speaking to this reality, Paul is saying something profoundly important about the necessity to "habitually be reordering [our] behavior within the sphere and by means of the Spirit."[3] John Piper gives us insight into what is required to habitually be reordering our behavior when he writes, "I have never been one of those who found his heart shrivel as God and his Word are known better. Putting more knowledge in my head about God and his way was like throwing wood in the furnace of my worship."[4]

Later in his book *Think*, Piper makes this critical observation: "That is what I have in mind by thinking—working hard with our minds to figure out meaning from texts. Then, of course, we go on from there to think how that meaning relates to other meanings in other texts and from experience in life. On and on the mind goes, until we build a coherent view of the world so that we can live a life that is rooted in a true understanding of God's Word and its application to the world."[5] That, by the way, is a great definition of disciple making.

I hope you caught that simple phrase "on and on the mind goes until." That captures the essence of the word *habitually*. It is something we do on and on until we arrive at a particular place and then continue so as to deepen our understanding of and commitment to something of great importance. Doing that takes effort, lots and lots of effort over a long period of time—actually, over an entire lifetime. There is no letup to this process.

Yet today I hear it said from virtually every corner of the church that, "No one, especially men, reads books anymore." "You can't keep people's attention for longer than thirty minutes." Or, one of my favorites, "People's attention spans have been shortened by too much screen time."

All of those observations have some basis in reality. It is, however, the very cultural reality that we are told by Paul to resist. So, why do we not listen to the great apostle's words? Why has the church allowed itself to be crushed into the mold of the world? Why have we not worked more diligently to help those who are part of our local assemblies to develop more fully the mind of Christ than the mind of the culture? That isn't intended to be a rhetorical question. I'd really like an answer that isn't just a shrug of the shoulders and a "Well, that's just the way it is." As the church of Jesus Christ, we aren't really given that option.

Even though I did not intend that to be a rhetorical question, I will go ahead and give an answer of my own. I think that we are just a bit too afraid of the level of effort it would take to actually engage in the challenging work of making disciples, and we are often too afraid of the resistance we might feel in response to our efforts. It's kind of the reason I resist trimming the trees in the wash behind my house. I know it will be a lot of work, it will be a bit dangerous, and I'm just not sure I want to take on such task. The difference between the one task and the other is, however, profound. Trimming tree limbs is useful. Disciple making is a mandate, one we don't get to ignore simply because it is too hard or will be met with resistance. The consequences of our failure to obey our Lord's clear commandment are apparent all around us. Yet still we resist.[6] Still we make excuses. Still we avert our eyes to what is readily apparent if we take but a moment to actually ponder what is happening all around us not only in the culture but in the church as well.

Permit me to finish with a few quick observations:

- The more seriously we take our responsibility to make disciples of the adults in our churches, the easier the task of discipling our children and young people will be.
- The more seriously we take our responsibility to make disciples of the adults in our churches, the greater positive impact we are likely to have on the surrounding culture.
- The more seriously we take our responsibility to make disciples of the adults in our churches, the more people in the culture will be drawn to Christ and His church.
- The more seriously we take our responsibility to make disciples of the adults in our churches, the more fully can we develop and employ the vast array of gifts given each of us by our Lord.
- The more seriously we take our responsibility to make disciples of the adults in our churches, the deeper will be our understanding of the Creator God, His creation, and our role in making that creation better.
- The more seriously we take our responsibility to make disciples of the adults in our churches, the richer will be our worship of Christ.
- The more seriously we take our responsibility to make disciples of the adults in our churches, the fewer members of our flock are likely to wander away and fall prey to the temptations of the world, the flesh, and the devil.
- The more seriously we take our responsibility to make disciples of the adults in our churches, the greater will be our compassion for the lost, for the dispossessed, for the marginalized, for the outsider, for the least of these, for the wounded among us.
- The more seriously we take our responsibility to make disciples of the adults in

our churches, the greater the probability that we will not turn a blind eye toward injustice.

- The more seriously we take our responsibility to make disciples of the adults in our churches, the more likely we will be to pray for our enemies and to seek reconciliation.

- The more seriously we take our responsibility to make disciples of the adults in our churches, . . . well, you fill in the blank.

In reality we can ill afford to ignore our responsibility to make disciples of all whom Christ has entrusted to our care. It is a task for which he holds us responsible and will one day ask us to give an accounting. What will we say then?

## For Reflection

1. Agree/disagree: The church is sometimes AWOL when it comes to challenging critical issues and events in our country. What could we do better in that regard? What keeps us from acting differently? What is it that we fear?

2. What would we need to do to help "build a coherent view of the world that is rooted in a true understanding of God's Word and its application to the world" into the hearts and minds of the children and adults in our churches? How are we doing in that regard?

3. Ponder and respond to the following: In reality we can ill-afford to ignore our responsibility to make disciples of all whom Christ has entrusted to our care.

# Notes

## Preface

1. James K. A. Smith, *You Are What You Love: The Spiritual Power of Habit*, Brazos Press, Grand Rapids, MI, 2016, p. 1.
2. Ibid., p. 2.
3. 2 John 1:4

## Introduction

1. *A Nation at Risk: The Imperative for Educational Reform: A Report to the Nation and the Secretary of Education*, United States Commission on Excellence in Education, 1983.
2. Barna Research: *State of the Church 2020; State of the Bible 2019; Six Reasons Young Christians Leave Church*, September 27, 2011; Earls, Aaron, *Most Teenagers Drop Out of Church as Young Adults*, Lifeway Research, March 22, 2020; Pew Research Center: *Though Still Conservative, Young Evangelicals Are More Liberal than Their Elders*, Jeff Diamat, May 4, 2017; Christian Smith and Melinda Lundquist Denton, *Soul Searching: The Religious and Spiritual Lives of American Teenagers*, Oxford University Press, NY, 2005; David Kinnaman, *You Lost Me: Why Young Christians Are Leaving the Church,* Baker Books, Grand Rapids, MI, 2011; Josh McDowell, *The Last Christian Generation: The Crisis Is Real. The Responsibility Is Ours*, Green Key Books, Holiday, FL, 2006; Stonestreet, John, "Why Young People Leave the Church and Why They Stay," Breakpoint Daily, February 25, 2020; Cox, Daniel, Thomson-DeVeaux, "Millennials Are Leaving Religion and Not Coming Back," fivethirtyeight.com, December 12, 2019.
3. Kidner, Derek, *Proverbs: An Introduction and Commentary*, IVP, Downers Grove, IL, 1964, 45.
4. Dryer, Rod, *The Benedict Option: A Strategy for Christians in a Post-Christian Nation*, Penguin Random House, New York, NY, 2017, 8.

## Chapter 1—Your Mission, Should You Decide to Accept It

1. Acts 1:8.
2. MacArthur, John, *The MacArthur New Testament Commentary: Matthew 24–28*, Moody Press, Chicago, 1989, 340.
3. Ibid, p. 345.
4. Ibid, p. 345.
5. Blamires, Harry, *The Christian Mind: How Should a Christian Think?*, Servant Books, Ann Arbor, MI, 1963, 3.
6. Malik, Charles, cited in *Love Your God with All Your Mind: The Role of Reason in the Life of the Soul*, Moreland, J.P., NavPress, Colorado Springs, 1997, 29.
7. Ibid, p. 29.
8. Macaulay, Ranald and Barrs, Jerram, *On Being Human: The Nature of Spiritual Experience*, IVP, 1978.
9. Carson, D. A., *The Gospel According to John*, IVP, Leicester, England and William Eerdmans Publishing Company, Grand Rapids, MI, 1991, 558.
10. Ephesians 6:4.

## Chapter 2—It Is Possible—If

1. MacArthur, John, *The MacArthur New Testament Commentary*: 2 Timothy, Moody Press, Chicago, IL, 1995, 167–68.
2. Piper, John, Ephesians 6:4, *Desiring God*, June 20, 2007; see as well Piper, John, "Public, Private, Online, Homeschool," desiring God.org.
3. Ibid.
4. Tarnass, Richard, *The Passions of the Western Mind: Understanding the Ideas that Have Shaped Our World View*, Ballantine Books, New York, NY, 1991, 29–30.
5. Noll, Mark, *The Scandal of the Evangelical Mind*, Wm. B. Eerdmans, Grand Rapids, MI, 1994.
6. Piper, Ibid.
7. Psalm 1:1–2.
8. Ephesians 4:11–17.
9. MacArthur, John, *The MacArthur New Testament Commentary: Ephesians*, Moody Press, Chicago, IL, 1986, 158.
10. Boice, James, *Ephesians: An Expositional Commentary*, Zondervan, Grand Rapids, MI, 1988, 133.

11. Garber, Steven, *The Fabric of Faithfulness: Weaving Together Belief and Behavior During the University Years*, IVP, Downers Grove, IL, 1996, 82.

## Chapter 3—It Is Required of a Steward

1. Ball, William, *Mere Creatures of the State: Education, Religion, and the Courts*, Crisis Books, Notre Dame, IN, 1994, 12.
2. Ibid, p. 12.
3. Ibid, p. 13.
4. 1 Peter 4:10.
5. Ps. 127:3.
6. MacArthur, John, *The MacArthur New Testament Commentary: 1 Corinthians*, Moody Press, Chicago, IL, 1984, 98.
7. Philippians 2:1–5.
8. See 1 Corinthians 4:2.
9. MacArthur, p. 99.
10. 1 Peter 5:1–5.
11. Matthew 25:14–30.
12. Amos 3:3.
13. Romans 8:19–23.
14. Romans 8:37.
15. For an in-depth look at shepherding, I would recommend *A Shepherd Looks at the Twenty-Third Psalm*, Philip Keller, Zondervan, Grand Rapids, MI, 1984.
16. A study of John chapter 10 would be informative and helpful.
17. Proverbs 27:23.
18. Tripp, Tedd, *Shepherding a Child's Heart*, Shepherd Press, Wapwallopen, PA, 1995, xix.
19. Ibid.
20. John 10:4.
21. 1 Samuel 17:34–36.
22. Acts 20:28–29.
23. Baut, Greg, *Education, Family, Law, California Family Council*, November 11, 2019, January 27, 2020, articles on California law SB-329 regarding sex education in California public schools.
24. Ibid.

25. Psalm 23:2.
26. Swindoll, Chuck, *Living Beyond the Daily Grind*, Book 1, Word Publishing, Dallas, TX, 1988, 73.
27. Psalm 23:4.
28. Swindoll, p. 77.
29. Kidner, *Proverbs: A Commentary*, IVP, Wheaton, IL, 51.
30. Joshua 24.
31. Palmer, Arnold, *A Life Well Played: My Stories*, St. Martins Press, New York, NY, 2016, x.
32. Ibid.
33. Deuteronomy 6.
34. Smith, Christian, Denton, Melinda Lundquist, *Soul Searching: The Religious and Spiritual Lives of American Teenagers*, Oxford University Press, New York, NY, 2005, 172–173.
35. 1 Samuel 17:20.

## Chapter 4—The Why Behind the What

1. Eliot, T. S., "The Aims of Education," in *To Criticize a Critic*, Farrar, Strano, and Giroux, New York, NY, 75-76.
2. *The Purpose of Education*, AZ Quotes.com.
3. Garber, Steven, *The Fabric of Faithfulness: Weaving Together Belief and Behavior During the University Years*, IVP, Downers Grove, IL, 1996, 69.
4. Noonan, Peggy, *Wall Street Journal*, Saturday, July 27, 2019.
5. Cited in *A History of Christian School Education*, Kienel, Paul A., Purposeful Design Publications, Colorado Springs, 1998, 167.
6. Ibid, p. 168.
7. Ibid, p. 167.
8. Kidner, Derek, *Proverbs: An Introduction and Commentary*, IVP, Downers Grove, IL, 1964, 13.
9. See Proverbs 1:7.
10. Packer, J. I., *Knowing God*, IVP, Downers Grove, IL, 1973.
11. Smith, James K. A., *You Are What You Love: The Spiritual Power of Habit*, Brazos Press, Grand Rapids, MI, 2016, 38.
12. Plato, *Republic*, Chapter 7, The Learning Revolution Project, brainyquote.com.

13. Lockerbie, D. Bruce, *Thinking and Acting Like a Christian: Love the Lord Your God with All Your Mind*, Multnomah Press, Portland, OR, 1989, 52.

14. Proverbs 14:15.

15. Proverbs 13:20.

16. Proverbs 18:2–3.

17. Proverbs 18:12–13, 15.

18. See again the text of Psalm 1.

## Chapter 5—Weaving the Fabric of Faithfulness

1. 1 Corinthians 9:27.

2. If you want to dig a little deeper into the how of teaching effectively, here is a short list of books that will help you begin that process. *Teaching Redemptively*, Donavan Graham; *Teaching to Change Lives*, Howard Hendricks; *A Christian Paideia*, D. Bruce Lockerbie; *By Design*, Martha E. McCullough; *Effective Bible Teaching*, Jim Wilhoit and Leland Ryken; *On Christian Teaching*, David I. Smith; *Recovering the Lost Tools of Learning*, Douglas Wilson.

3. Hendricks, Howard, *Teaching to Change Lives*, Multnomah Press, Portland, OR, 1987, 27.

4. Lockerbie, D. Bruce, *Thinking and Acting Like a Christian*, Multnomah Press, Portland, OR, 1989, 52.

5. *The Fabric of Faithfulness*, Steven Garber, IVP, Downers Grove, IL, 1996, 19–20.

6. See research by Dr. Christian Smith, *Soul Searching: The Spiritual and Religious Lives of American Teenagers*; Josh McDowell, *The Last Christian Generation*; David Kinnaman, *You Lost Me: Why Young Christians Are Leaving the Church*; James K. A. Smith, *Desiring the Kingdom*; David P. Setran and Chris A. Kiesling, *Spiritual Formation in Emerging Adulthood*.

7. Ibid.

8. Egan, Timothy, *The Worst Hard Time: The Untold Story of Those Who Survived the Great American Dust Bowl*, Mariner Book, Boston/NY, 2006, 34.

9. Ibid.

10. Ibid.

11. Ibid.

12. Garber, Steven, *The Fabric of Faithfulness: Weaving Together Belief and Behavior During the University Years*, IVP, Downers Grove, IL, 1996, 88.

13. Ibid.
14. Smith, Christian and Denton, Melinda Lundquist, *Soul Searching: The Religious and Spiritual Lives of American Teenagers*, Oxford University Press, New York, NY, 2005, 172.
15. Ibid, p. 173.
16. Ibid, p. 137.
17. Isaiah 5:20–21; see as well Romans 1:18–23, where Paul talks of those who "suppress the truth."
18. Matthew 18:5–6: Ephesians 4:14.

## Chapter 6—More Threads, More Weaving

1. Ecclesiastes 7:15; 8:14.
2. Garber, Steven, *The Fabric of Faithfulness: Weaving Together Belief and Behavior During the University Years*, IVP, Downers Grove, IL, 1996, 111.
3. Acts 26:24.
4. Acts 26:25–26.
5. See 1 Corinthians 15:1–19 for the full context.
6. 1 John 1:1–3.
7. 2 Peter 1:16.
8. John Stonestreet, *BreakPoint*, October 4, 2019.
9. Moreland, J. P. *Love Your God with All Your Mind; The Role of Reason in the Life of the Soul*, Colorado Springs. NavPress, 1997, 75–76.
10. Smith, Christian, and Denton, Melinda Lundquist, *Soul Searching: The Religious and Spiritual Lives of American Teenagers*, Oxford University Press, NY, 2005, 130.
11. Ibid, p. 130.
12. Ibid, p. 131.
13. Ibid, p. 130.
14. 1 Peter 3:13–17.
15. Robert Lewis, *The Church of Irresistible Influence*, Zondervan, Grand Rapids, MI, 2001, 40-41.
16. See 1 Timothy 3:1–13.
17. See James and 1 John.
18. 1 John 3:11–18; see James 3:14-18.

19. Dr. Steven Garber shared this definition of integrity at a CCCU presentation. He described someone with integrity as a person whose external, public behavior is fully aligned with their internal beliefs.

20. Lencioni, Patrick, *The Advantage: Why Organizational Health Trumps Everything Else in Business*, Jossey-Bass, San Francisco, CA, 2012, 5.

21. Matthew 23:2–3.

## Chapter 7—The Final Threads

1. Matthew 22:37.

2. Garber, Steven, *The Fabric of Faithfulness: Weaving Together Belief and Behavior During the University Years*, IVP, Downers Grove, IL, 141.

3. Ibid, p. 142.

4. Matthew 23:37.

5. Matthew 23:38.

6. Proverbs 22:6.

7. Kidner, Derek, *Proverbs: An Introduction and Commentary*, IVP, Downers Grove, IL, 1964, 147.

8. 1 Corinthians 15:33. See as well Solomon's warning to his son on the impact of bad companions, Proverbs 1:8–19.

9. Bellah, Robert, et al, *Habits of the Heart: Individualism and Commitment in American Life*, University of California Press, Berkley, CA, 1985, 84.

10. Romans 12:21.

11. Bella, Ibid., p. 84.

12. Hebrews 10:23–25.

13. Turkel, Sherry, *Alone Together: Why We Expect More from Technology and Less from Each Other*, Basic Books, New York, NY, 2011, 239.

14. Bonhoeffer, Dietrich, *Called to Community: The Life Jesus Wants for His People*, quote from Quotetab.com.

15. Read the full account in Acts 9.

16. Hebrews 11:32–39.

17. Hebrews 11:13–16.

18. Proverbs 1:7.

19. Kidner, Derek, *Proverbs: An Introduction and Commentary*, IVP, Downers Grove, IL, 1964, 59.

20. 1 Corinthians 15:31.
21. 1 Corinthians 9:27.
22. Romans 12:1–2.
23. Collins, Jim, *Good to Great: Why Some Companies Make the Leap . . . and Others Don't*, Harper Business, New York, NY, 2001, 198. For fuller insight into the concept of the genius of AND, see Collins, Jim, and Porras, Jerry, *Built to Last: Successful Habits of Highly Visionary Companies*, Harper Business, New York, NY, 1994, 43–45.
24. Smith, James K. A., *Desiring the Kingdom: Worship, Worldview, and Cultural Formation*, Baker Books, Grand Rapids, MI, 2009.

## Chapter 8—Questions That Must Be Asked

1. To illustrate this point, see an interesting article by John Stonestreet in the May 13, 2020 issue of *BreakPoint Daily* from the Colson Center titled, "No Lord of the Flies Scenario with These Christian Boys." Consider this observation from that article. "Underneath the story of these real-life boys from Tonga is the fact that they were formed, at their boarding school and likely elsewhere too, by a Christian faith and worldview. As scholar and author Anthony Esolen wrote on Facebook in response to this story, 'religious faith is the strongest bond for any human society, especially when times are tough.'"
2. Semmelweis Society International.
3. See 2 Timothy 3:16–17. And, by the way, the "all Scripture" to which Paul refers in this text primarily refers to the Old Testament. The idea that the church today should "decouple" itself from the Old Testament is dangerous and disingenuous.

## Chapter 9—More Assertions, More Answers

1. Cited in "The Viral Pandemic and Distrust and Misinformation," *BreakPoint Daily*, John Stonestreet with Shane Morris, April 17, 2020.
2. Oppenheimer, Todd, *The Flickering Mind: The False Promise of Technology in the Classroom and How Learning Can Be Saved*, Random House, New York, NY, 2003, 395.
3. Dreher, Rod, *The Benedict Option: A Strategy for Christians in a Post-Christian Nation*, Sentinel, New York, NY, 2017, 147.
4. 2 Corinthians 10:3–5.

5. Colossians 2:8.
6. Romans 12:2.
7. Proverbs 22:15.
8. Ephesians 6:4.
9. Matthew 18:3–6.
10. Luke 6:39–40.
11. Stark, Rodney, *The Triumph of Christianity: How the Jesus Movement Became the World's Largest Religion*, Harper One, New York, NY, 2011, 116–118.

## Chapter 10—How Did We Get Here?

1. Padover, Samuel K. Editor, 1939, *Democracy by Thomas Jefferson*, New York, Appleton Century Press. Quoted in Pue, Alan, "The Significance of the Recent Reemergence of Evangelical/Fundamentalist Christian Schools," EdD diss., University of Delaware, 1986.
2. McCarthy, Skillen, and Harper. 1982. *Disestablishment a Second Time: Genuine Pluralism for American Schools*. Grand Rapids, MI, Eerdmans, 49. Cited in Pue, Alan, "The Significance of the Recent Reemergence of Evangelical/Fundamentalist Christian Schools," EdD diss., University of Delaware, 1986.
3. James Sire, from the introduction to *The God Who Is There*, Francis Schaeffer, Inter-Varsity Press, Downers Grove, IL, 14–15.
4. Peterson, Eugene H., *Run with the Horses: The Quest for Life at Its Best*, Inter-Varsity Press, Downers Grove, IL, 1983, 37–38.
5. The following short list (in no particular order) should get you started. Nancy Pearcey, *Total Truth: Liberating Christianity from Its Cultural Captivity*; D. Bruce Lockerbie, *Thinking and Acting Like a Christian, A Passion for Learning, A Christian Paideia, Dismissing God, The Cosmic Center*; Albert E. Greene, *Reclaiming the Future of Christian Education*; J. Gresham Machen, *Education, Christianity and the State*; McCarthy, Oppewal, Peterson, Spykman, *Society, State and Schools*; McCarthy, Skillen, Harper, *Disestablishment a Second Time: Genuine Pluralism for American Schools*; William Ball, *Mere Creatures of the State*; Ashley Rogers Berner, *No One Way to School: Pluralism and American Public Education*; Frank Gaebelein, *Christian Education in a Democracy*; John Richard Neuhaus, *Democracy and the Renewal of Public Education, The Naked Public Square*; Rousas John Rushdoony, *The Messianic Character of American Education*; David Gelernter, *America-Lite: How Imperial Academia Dismantled Our Culture*;

Dinesh D'Souza, *Illiberal Education: The Politics and Race and Sex on Campus*; Thomas Sowell, *Inside American Education*; Robert K. Carlson, *Truth on Trial*; Paul D. Spears, Steven R. Loomis, *Education for Human Flourishing*; Robert L. Cord, *The Separation of Church and State: Historic Fact and Current Fiction*.

6. Joel Belz, *World Magazine*, March 14, 2020, Volume 35 Number 6, 10.

7. Ibid, p. 10.

8. Schaeffer, Francis, *The God Who Is There*, InterVarsity Press, Downers Grove, IL, 1st edition, 1968, 25–26.

9. Romans 12:1–2.

10. Rockne, M. McCarthy, Skillen, James W., Harper, William A., *Disestablishment a Second Time: Genuine Pluralism for American Schools*, Wm. B. Eerdmans, Grand Rapid, MI, 1982, 60.

11. Cremin, Lawrence, *Traditions of American Education*, Basic Books, New York, NY, 1977, 80.

12. Mead, Sidney, *Lively Experiment: The Shaping of Christianity in America*, Harper and Row, New York, NY, 1963, 69.

13. Here are some resources on the Irish immigrant experience in the USA. *The Immortal Irishman: The Irish Revolutionary Who Became an American Hero*, Timothy Egan; *Emigrants and Exiles: Ireland and the Irish Exodus to North America*, Kirby A. Miller; "When America Despised the Irish: The 19th Century Refugee Crisis," Christopher Klein, History.com.

14. Blumenfeld, Samuel L, *Is Public Education Necessary?* The Paradigm Company, Boise, ID, 185.

15. McCarthy, Skillen, and Harper, 58.

16. Ibid, p. 54.

17. For a fuller understanding of deism I would recommend James Sire's book *The Universe Next Door*, IVP, Downers Grove, IL.

## Chapter 11—Where Do We Go from Here?

1. Oshinsky, David, "When Epidemics Wreaked Havoc in America," *Wall Street Journal*, March 11, 2020.

2. Cox, Daniel and Thomson-DeVeaux, Amelia, "Millennials Are Leaving Religion and Not Coming Back," fivethirtyeight.com, December 12, 2019.

3. Stonestreet, John, "Why Young People Leave the Church—and Why They Stay," *BreakPoint Daily*, February 25, 2020.

4. Ibid.

5. Ibid.

6. Modarelli, Brian, "Navigating the Cardus Education Survey," *CSE Magazine.*

7. Ibid. For both pastors and parents I would strongly recommend that you read the full executive summary of the Cardus Education Survey—not just because the research was exceptional, which it was, but because it is actual research and not just the kind of anecdotal evidence that gets shared among pastors and parents.

8. This occurred in a private conversation at Prestonwood Christian Academy in Dallas, Texas, that I was privileged to attend with a small group of school leaders.

9. Proverbs 29:19.

10. Hebrews 10:24.

11. Moreland, J. P., *Love Your God with All Your Mind: The Role of Reason in the Life of the Soul*, NavPress, Colorado Springs, CO, 1997.

12. For an interesting look at that reality read John Grisham's *The Painted House*, which is a fascinating exegesis of small-town America in the early 1950s.

13. Here are just a few articles speaking to the efforts of teacher unions to oppose charter and private schools. "School Opening Extortion: Teacher Unions Are Using Covid 19 as a Political Weapon," *WSJ*, August 3, 2020; "The Battle Over Charter Schools," Zachary Jason, *Harvard Education Magazine*, Summer 2017; "Charter Schools Are a Flashpoint in California's Teacher Strikes," Ricardo Cain, February 22, 2019: CalMatters; "The Implacable Resistance to Charter Schools," Charles Chiappo, September 28, 2015, Governing: The Future of State and Localities; *Liberating Learning: Technology, Politics, and the Future of American Education*, Chubb, John E. and Moe, Terry M., Josey-Bass, San Francisco, CA, 2009.

14. Stott, John, *Christian Counter-Culture: The Message of the Sermon on the Mount*, IVP, Downers Grove, IL, 1978, 17.

15. Here are three organizations that provide encouragement and instruction for Christian teachers in government-funded public schools: Christian Educators Association, Teachers Who Pray, and Teach 4 the Heart.

16. Read and ponder James 1:22–25, 2:14–16, and 1 John 3:16–18.

17. Sproul, R. C. "Christ and Culture, Tolerance and Conviction," found in *Classical Apologetics*, Zondervan, Grand Rapids, MI, 1984, 4.

18. See articles on Espinoza v Montana Department of Revenue, the 2020 US Supreme Court decision related to government funding of private and religious schools: Opinion Analysis, Amy Howe, SCOTUS Blog; *National Review*, June

30, 2020, Espinoza Ends State-Sanctioned Religious Discrimination in Education, Andrea Piciotti-Bayer, June 30, 2020.

19. "Brethren of the Common Life," Wikipedia.

20. "Brethren of the Common Life," editors of *The Encyclopaedia Britannica*.

21. Hunter, James Davidson, *To Change the World: The Irony, Tragedy, and Possibility of Christianity in the Late Modern World*, Oxford University Press, 2010, 4.

22. Ibid, p. 57.

23. Ibid, p. 54.

24. See Daniel 1:3–4.

25. Baldwin, Joyce G., *Daniel: An Introduction and Commentary*, Tyndale Old Testament Commentaries, D.J. Wiseman, General Editor, IVP, Downers Grove, IL, 1978, 80.

26. Ibid, p. 80.

27. Ibid, pp. 80–81.

## Afterword

1. Ephesians 4:11–17.

2. Romans 12:1–2. See as well Matthew 22:37, where Jesus calls his followers to love God with their mind as well as with their heart.

3. Wuest, Kenneth, *Romans in the Greek New Testament*, William B. Eerdmans Publishing Company, Grand Rapids, MI, 208.

4. Piper, John, *Think: The Life of the Mind and the Love of God*, Crossway, Wheaton, IL, 2010, 26.

5. Ibid, p. 45.

6. I would encourage you to read two books that help illuminate our current challenges in what we still call the "evangelical" church, a descriptor that is increasingly useless if our goal is to identify churches that truly embrace and advance the gospel of Christ. The first is *Christianity and Liberalism* written by the great Princeton theologian J. Gresham Machen. In that book Machen, observing the sorry state of the "confessing" church, argued that liberalism had abandoned historic Christian truth. More recently, *Another Gospel: A Lifelong Christian Seeks Truth in Response to Progressive Christianity*, authored by Alisa Childers, takes up the same topic. Machen's book was written for theologians. Childers's book is written with a more popular audience in mind. It, however, makes a compelling case for the authority of Scripture and the truth of the gospel.

It's Time to **Flourish**

What legacy do you want to leave for the students that sit in your classrooms?

ACSI wants to come alongside you and help build a plan for your school community to flourish how God intends—biblically. Engage with us on a new journey of flourishing at acsi.org/flourishing.

"May the LORD cause you to flourish,
both you and your children."
Psalm 115:14

# Also Available From Purposeful Design Publications

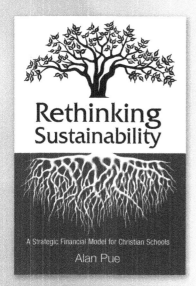

Are you concerned about the sustainability of your school? Dr. Pue's insights, warnings, and advice can help your school not only survive, but thrive!

Alan Pue concentrates decades of teaching, leading, and consulting into this passionate plea to leaders of Christian schools—along with a proven plan for success.